STERLING BIOGRAPHIES

HELEN KELLER

Courage in Darkness

Emma Carlson Berne

STERLING

New York / London
www.sterlingpublishing.com/kids

For my own teachers: Mom and Dad

STERLING and the distinctive Sterling logo are registered trademarks of Sterling Publishing Co., Inc.

Library of Congress Cataloging-in-Publication Data
Berne, Emma Carlson.
  Helen Keller : courage in darkness / Emma Carlson Berne.
    p. cm. — (Sterling biographies)
  Includes bibliographical references and index.
  ISBN 978-1-4027-5147-9 (pbk.) — ISBN 978-1-4027-6541-4 (hardcover)
  1. Keller, Helen, 1880–1968—Juvenile literature. 2. Deafblind women—United States—Biography—Juvenile literature. 3. Sullivan, Annie, 1866–1936—Juvenile literature. I. Title.
  HV1624.K4B44 2009
  362.4'1092—dc22
  [B]
                              2008032680

10 9 8 7 6 5 4 3 2 1

Published by Sterling Publishing Co., Inc.
387 Park Avenue South, New York, NY 10016
© 2009 by Emma Carlson Berne

Distributed in Canada by Sterling Publishing
c/o Canadian Manda Group, 165 Dufferin Street
Toronto, Ontario, Canada M6K 3H6
Distributed in the United Kingdom by GMC Distribution Services
Castle Place, 166 High Street, Lewes, East Sussex, England BN7 1XU
Distributed in Australia by Capricorn Link (Australia) Pty. Ltd.
P.O. Box 704, Windsor, NSW 2756, Australia

Printed in China
All rights reserved

Sterling ISBN 978-1-4027-5147-9 (paperback)
          ISBN 978-1-4027-6541-4 (hardcover)

Image research by Larry Schwartz

For information about custom editions, special sales, premium and corporate purchases, please contact Sterling Special Sales Department at 800-805-5489 or specialsales@sterlingpublishing.com.

Contents

Events in the Life of Helen Keller

1880

1968

June 27, 1880
Helen Keller is born to Captain Arthur and Kate Keller in Tuscumbia, Alabama.

March 3, 1887
Annie Sullivan arrives in Tuscumbia, Alabama.

May 1888
Helen, Mrs. Keller, and Sullivan travel to Boston to visit the Perkins Institution for the Blind and meet Michael Anagnos.

Fall 1894
Accompanied by Sullivan, Keller enters the Wright-Humason School for the Deaf in New York.

October 1896
Keller enters the Cambridge School for Young Ladies in order to prepare for the Radcliffe College entrance exams.

1903
Keller's first memoir, *The Story of My Life*, is published with the help of John Macy.

1906
Keller is appointed to the Massachusetts Commission for the Blind.

1913
Keller goes on her first lecture tour.

1914
Annie Sullivan and John Macy separate; Polly Thomson is hired as assistant and secretary.

1919
Keller and Sullivan make their first appearance on the vaudeville circuit.

November 1921
Kate Keller dies.

April 1930
Keller, Sullivan, and Thomson travel to Scotland, England, and Ireland on their first trip abroad.

April 1, 1937
Keller and Thomson travel to Japan for the first time. Keller is very popular among the Japanese people and would maintain a lifelong relationship with Japan.

March 21, 1960
Polly Thomson dies. Evelyn Seide and Winifred Corbally take over as Keller's caretakers.

June 1, 1968
Helen Keller dies at home in her sleep at Arcan Ridge in Westport, Connecticut, a few days after suffering a heart attack.

February 1882
Keller contracts a childhood illness that leaves her blind and deaf.

April 5, 1887
Helen has a breakthrough when she makes a connection at the pump house between the word *water* and the sensation of water running over her hand.

November 4, 1891
Keller mails "The Frost King" to Michael Anagnos and is later accused of plagiarism.

August 19, 1896
Captain Arthur Keller dies.

Fall 1900
Keller enters Radcliffe College as the nation's first deaf-blind college student.

June 28, 1904
Keller graduates from Radcliffe College.

May 2, 1905
Annie Sullivan marries John Macy in Wrentham, Massachusetts.

1909
Keller joins the Socialist Party and becomes a Socialist activist.

1916
Helen Keller and Peter Fagan take out a marriage license in Boston, Massachusetts, but separate before they can marry.

August 1919
Deliverance, a film based on Keller's life, premieres in New York at the Lyric Theater.

1924
Keller begins fund-raising work for the American Foundation for the Blind.

October 20, 1936
Annie Sullivan Macy dies. Keller is devastated at Sullivan's death and retreats to Europe with Polly Thomson.

1941
As wounded soldiers from World War II begin appearing in U.S. hospitals, Keller and Thomson start to visit blinded and maimed veterans.

September 14, 1964
Keller receives the Presidential Medal of Freedom.

Commencement

College has breathed new life into my mind and given me new views of things, a perception of new truths and of new aspects of the old ones.

On June 28, 1904, ninety-six young women filed into an auditorium at Radcliffe College. The graduating seniors had worked hard for four years to achieve a college education. Only one made history that day: Helen Keller became the first deaf-blind person to be awarded a bachelor of arts degree.

As she mounted the steps of the stage, her teacher Annie Sullivan by her side, the murmuring crowd grew quiet. Moving with assurance, she crossed to the podium, and with her outstretched hand accepted the diploma placed in it. Even though she could not hear it, applause rippled through the audience.

Seventeen years before, Helen Keller had been a wild, uncontrollable child, trapped in silence and darkness. She could not read or write. She could not express herself with language. Now Helen was not only a college graduate, but also she was a confident young woman with a keen social awareness and a ready sense of humor.

Helen Keller's graduation from Radcliffe College was only one event in her long, varied life. She was an author, an advocate for blind people, a fund-raiser, a political activist, a vaudeville performer, and a silent-movie star. Through her convictions, she showed the world that people with disabilities should not—and would not—be pushed aside.

CHAPTER 1

Life in Darkness

[T]his child has more sense than all the Kellers—
if there is any way to reach her mind.

—Helen's Aunt Ev

Helen Keller's birth must have seemed a perfectly ordinary event. The first daughter of Arthur and Kate Keller was born healthy and strong on June 27, 1880, in the small, rural town of Tuscumbia, Alabama. The Keller home, Ivy Green, was a beautiful, tranquil place. Located on six hundred forty acres, the rambling white-clapboard house

This photograph shows Ivy Green, the Keller family home in Tuscumbia, Alabama, as it appears today. It has been preserved for visitors, who can tour the house and the grounds.

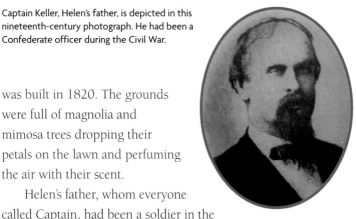

Captain Keller, Helen's father, is depicted in this nineteenth-century photograph. He had been a Confederate officer during the Civil War.

was built in 1820. The grounds were full of magnolia and mimosa trees dropping their petals on the lawn and perfuming the air with their scent.

Helen's father, whom everyone called Captain, had been a soldier in the Confederate army during the Civil War and was a proud southerner. He was an avid hunter who loved his bird dogs like family members. Though Captain Keller came from an old southern family and was trained as a lawyer, he struggled to make ends meet after the war ended. Keller planted cotton to sell and edited a small newspaper called *North Alabamian*.

Kate Adams Keller was a young woman from Memphis, Tennessee, when she married the forty-two-year-old Captain Keller. Though Kate was also a southerner and her father a Confederate soldier, Kate's roots were in the north. Her father had been born in Massachusetts, and the family was related to the famous founding father John Adams.

Kate Adams Keller, Helen's mother, is shown seated in this formal photograph. She was raised in the South, but her father was from the northern state of Massachusetts.

Life was probably not easy for the pampered young Kate after her marriage. Many southerners fought poverty and economic hardship during **Reconstruction** and the period immediately afterward. The people of Tuscumbia were no exception. The Keller family was comfortable but not well-off and could not afford to keep very many servants. Kate spent her days tending the large vegetable garden on which the family depended, raising chickens, ducks, and turkeys, doing dishes, boiling water for laundry, and making her own butter, lard, and bacon from the livestock on the farm.

Life-Changing Illness

Even when she was a baby, Helen's family could tell that their daughter was smart. At the age of six months, Helen could already say "How d'ye" ("How do you do?"), "tea," and "wah-wah" for *water*. Soon she was able to toddle after her mother, probably clinging to her mother's skirt as Kate went about her household duties. Like most babies, Helen probably spent her days exploring the new, fresh world. She no doubt played with spoons, pots and pans, and wooden rattles. It is easy to imagine her running on little feet from one end of the house to the other, occasionally tumbling over a stool or a shoe in her path. However, these happy, exciting days ended in February 1882 when Helen was nineteen months old.

Helen had become ill with what was probably scarlet fever. Helen's own doctor recorded that she had a "severe congestion of the stomach and brain," and that she had "brain fever." Some historians believe this sickness was meningitis; most believe scarlet fever was the likely culprit.

In the days before routine immunizations, children frequently became ill with sometimes-serious diseases, such as measles,

Scarlet Fever and Meningitis

Both of the diseases suspected of causing Helen's disabilities are serious illnesses. Scarlet fever is caused by a bacterial infection. The sick person develops a sore throat, a fever, a distinct red rash on the body, and a swollen, bright-red tongue. Today, scarlet fever is easily treatable with antibiotics, but in Helen's time it could be fatal. Scarlet fever is also highly contagious. During the nineteenth century and into the twentieth century, patients were often kept in isolation hospitals or **quarantined** at home. Helen's doctor may have prescribed treatments such as sponge baths, gargling, and **poultices** applied to the neck—all of which would have been virtually useless in controlling the disease.

Meningitis, the other disease Helen may have had, is just as dangerous as scarlet fever. People who have meningitis usually have a high fever, feel tired, and have a stiff neck and a skin rash. Today, meningitis is treated with antibiotics, steroids, and intravenous fluids. Back in the nineteenth century, there was almost no treatment for meningitis. Helen's doctor might have applied ice to her head to bring down her fever and perhaps gave her **opium** if she seemed like she was in pain.

Quarantines were used regularly to curb the spread of scarlet fever, both in Helen's childhood and later in the twentieth century. This photograph from the 1950s depicts a sign warning that a scarlet-fever quarantine is in effect.

mumps, diphtheria, whooping cough, meningitis, and scarlet fever. There were few effective treatments for these illnesses. All parents could do was put their children to bed, watch, and wait.

For several days, Helen lay in bed, desperately ill. Her family was sure she would die. Miraculously, Helen did not. Gradually, her fever went down and her restless body grew still. Helen's parents must have breathed a sigh of relief that their little girl had been spared.

However, all was not well. Many years later, Helen herself remembered that after her illness, her eyes hurt her and felt dry and hot. One day during Helen's illness, her half-brother James lifted her in his arms from the sofa where she was lying. As soon as her face was raised up, she screamed as if the light hurt her eyes. The day that Kate Keller passed her hand in front of her little girl's eyes and Helen did not blink, she knew that Helen had become blind.

When Helen did not flinch at the loud clanging of a dinner bell, then the Kellers realized the full truth: Helen was deaf and blind at nineteen months. She would remain so for the rest of her life.

The Wild Child.

Although Helen was locked in a box of darkness and silence, she could still communicate. As she grew over the years, she developed sixty signs to express herself: putting on glasses and pretending to read a newspaper was the sign for her father, patting her cheek indicated her mother, sucking her thumb meant her new baby sister, Mildred. When she wanted her mother to make ice cream, Helen made the cranking motion of the ice cream churn and shivered.

Helen was a sturdy, robust child who was bursting to know the world around her. She could run and play all day without

Deaf-blindness Today

Many children during the 1800s, such as Helen Keller, were deaf and blind because of illnesses contracted in childhood. Today, however, many of those same illnesses have either been destroyed or are treatable with medicine, so most deaf-blindness in modern times is not caused by disease. Many people who are deaf and blind today were born extremely premature, which can cause hearing and vision loss. Prematurity can also cause mental disability and developmental delays. Some hereditary syndromes can also cause deaf-blindness. In addition, many deaf-blind children today are not completely without hearing or sight, as Helen was. They might be able to see a little or hear a little. Most of the time, doctors and parents realize very soon after birth that the child is deaf-blind and immediately begin teaching the child how to function in a hearing-sighted world.

Most blind children today are taught Braille, the system of reading using raised dots in place of letters. This photograph shows an adult hand guiding a child's hand on a Braille label marking a bed of flowers.

In this photograph taken in 1887, Helen poses with her pet dog.

getting tired and was interested in everything that happened in the household. As Helen grew, so did her desire to communicate with people. She wanted to express herself, but she did not know how. She would throw horrible tantrums when she was frustrated, breaking dishes and throwing them across the room.

To make matters worse, the Kellers could not stand to deny their daughter anything she wanted. As a result, Helen became very spoiled. When she was refused anything, she would scratch, bite, and hit people. At meals, instead of remaining in her seat and eating her food, Helen would roam around the table, putting her hands into everyone's plates and taking whatever she liked.

Sometimes, Helen was actually dangerous. She locked her mother in the kitchen pantry one day while the rest of the household were out of doors and sat on the floor for three hours while her mother banged on the door.

She wanted to express herself, but she did not know how.

An even more serious incident occurred when Helen was five. She was terribly jealous of her new baby sister, Mildred. One day, Helen found the baby lying in her cradle by the fire. In a fit of temper, Helen overturned the cradle, intending to dump the baby on the floor. Kate flew across the room and managed to catch Mildred before she fell.

Helen had caught on that other people around her communicated by moving their mouths in certain ways. However, when she tried to imitate them by getting their attention and then moving her own mouth, it had no effect. Helen did not understand what speech was and how it was used.

Helen was growing older, and as her desire to communicate grew stronger, her tantrums grew stronger and more frequent. Her family members were covered in welts and bruises from her outbursts.

The Kellers were at a loss. Clearly the family could not go on like this. What should they do? Was Helen even capable of controlling herself? One of the Keller uncles thought that she was mentally disabled and should be sent to an institution for constant care. However, Helen's Aunt Ev, whom she adored, thought that "this child has more sense than all the Kellers—if there is any way to reach her mind." No matter what, everyone agreed: Something had to be done about Helen—soon.

In this 1888 photograph from the Perkins School for the Blind History Museum, an eight-year-old Helen poses with her baby sister, Mildred.

CHAPTER 2

Enter Annie

The most important day I remember in all my life is the one on which my teacher, Anne Mansfield Sullivan, came to me.

The doctors in Tuscumbia had told Helen's parents that she would never regain her hearing or sight. However, the Kellers refused to give up. Perhaps other doctors could help Helen—and if she could not be cured, perhaps she could be educated.

At some point, Kate Keller had read a book called *American Notes* by the famous popular author Charles Dickens. Dickens had written about the education of a deaf-blind girl, Laura Bridgman, at a school in Boston called the Perkins Institution for the Blind. Laura had contracted scarlet fever at the age of two, and the disease left her deaf, blind, **mute**, and without a sense of smell or taste. Using touch, the only sense she had left, a physician and teacher named Samuel Gridley Howe had taught Laura to communicate using a manual alphabet. Letters were represented by finger signs, which were spelled into Laura's hand. She could spell back in return. Dr. Howe had also taught Laura to read using raised type as well as to sew and make lace, among other skills. Kate realized, though, that the account she was reading was years old. Laura Bridgman was a grown woman now, and Dr. Howe was long dead.

Until reading about Laura Bridgman, the Kellers did not even know if it was possible to educate Helen at all.

In this artist's rendition c. 1838, Samuel Gridley Howe stands beside Laura Bridgman, his famous deaf-blind student. Laura is wearing the green eye covering that was typical of students of that time at the Perkins Institution.

They still did not—but at least now they had a glimmer of hope that she could be taught.

A Sign of Hope

The Kellers decided to take Helen to a famous oculist (a type of doctor that treats eye diseases) in Baltimore. Helen loved the long train ride and was quiet and attentive to all of the new things she felt around her. The oculist could do nothing for Helen's eyes, but he did suggest that the Kellers take Helen to visit Alexander Graham Bell in Washington, D.C. The famous inventor of the telephone had a deep personal interest in deaf people—his mother and wife were deaf, and Bell had worked for years to create assistive devices for deaf people. Helen liked the

Laura Bridgman in *American Notes*

In this excerpt from Charles Dickens's *American Notes*, the author describes meeting Laura Bridgman for the first time, when she was a young girl.

"Her face was radiant with intelligence and pleasure. Her hair, braided by her own hands, was bound about a head, whose intellectual capacity and development were beautifully expressed in its graceful outline, and its broad open brow; her dress, arranged by herself, was a pattern of neatness and simplicity; the work she had knitted, lay beside her; her writing-book was on the desk she leaned upon. —From the mournful ruin of such bereavement [the term Dickens used to describe Laura's disabilities], there had slowly risen up this gentle, tender, guileless, grateful-hearted being."

This photograph shows Laura Bridgman, still wearing her eye covering, as a teenager in 1845.

white-bearded man, who let her feel the vibrating ticking of his big pocket watch. While Helen sat on his knee, Bell suggested that the Kellers contact the Perkins Institution, the school Kate Keller had read about in *American Notes*—and Laura Bridgman's current home. Maybe the school director, Michael Anagnos, would be able to help them.

Hope no doubt flooded the hearts of the Kellers, and the Captain immediately wrote to Anagnos, asking him if he knew of a teacher who could come to Tuscumbia to live with them and teach Helen. She would live in their home as one of the family, and they would pay her well. Of course, this teacher would have to be a special sort of person: strong, tough, smart, and able to withstand Helen's rages and tantrums.

Anagnos received the letter in August 1886, but it was not until January 1887 that the anxious Kellers received the reply: Anagnos had found a teacher. Annie Sullivan would be arriving in Tuscumbia in two months.

This portrait of Annie Sullivan as a young woman shows how she might have looked when she first met Helen.

From the Depths of Poverty and Cruelty

Twenty-year-old Annie Sullivan could not have been more different from the cultured southern Kellers. Born into abject poverty in a village in Massachusetts, Annie's parents were Irish immigrants. Annie had four siblings, but only two lived past the age of five: her sister Mary and her brother Jimmie. Annie's mother died of **tuberculosis** when she was eight years old. Her father, Thomas, was an abusive alcoholic. Annie herself was a fiery, angry girl. She also had a chronic eye condition called trachoma, in which lumps on the underside of the eyelids scratched and irritated the eyes. The trachoma was gradually destroying Annie's vision, and from a young age she had learned to navigate in a world of blurred outlines and hazy colors.

After the death of her mother, Annie had only one person in the world she loved and cared for—her little brother Jimmie, who was born with a hip affected by tuberculosis and could walk only with a crutch. Annie and Jimmie clung to each other as their fragile world was dismantled after the death of their mother. Their father's drinking and rages were worse than ever, and the family was poverty-stricken. Mary was sent to live with well-off relatives, but no one wanted sick little Jimmie with his deformed hip or his angry, defiant, half-blind sister Annie.

Twenty-year-old Annie Sullivan could not have been more different from the cultured southern Kellers.

With nowhere else to go, Annie and Jimmie were sent to live in a poorhouse in the town of Tewksbury, Massachusetts. This was common in the days before social services. In the poorhouse, people who could not support themselves lived together with all sorts of others: prostitutes, alcoholics, criminals, people with disabilities, people who were mentally ill, often with everyone jumbled together in filthy conditions.

Jimmie died of his tuberculosis soon after the children arrived in Tewksbury, and Annie was driven almost mad with grief. For the rest of her life, she would never forget her little brother; and on her deathbed many years later, she would call out for him and remember that awful moment at the poorhouse when she saw his body laid out for burial. Without anyone else to turn to, Annie made friends with the young prostitutes and unwed mothers in Tewksbury, and over the years, grew to regard the place as her home.

Getting Out of Tewksbury

Annie, however, was not content. She was a smart girl. She had a keen intelligence that refused to stay quiet. She was receiving no education in Tewksbury, and what's more, no one cared. Annie cared. She wanted to go to school—more than anything—and to read and write and be with other girls her age. Annie was not the type to just sit quietly and wait for something to happen to her. If she were, she would probably have stayed at the poorhouse the rest of her days. Instead, when she was only about fourteen, Annie made a plan.

She heard that a distinguished group of

This nineteenth-century photograph shows Annie Sullivan as a teenager—at about the time she left Tewksbury to attend the Perkins Institution.

Frank Sanborn, the chairman of the State Board of Charities for Massachusetts, is depicted in this engraving from *Harper's New Monthly Magazine* in June 1875. Mr. Sanborn was responsible for Annie's eventual transfer from the poorhouse.

community leaders would be visiting the poorhouse and that among them would be Frank Sanborn, the chairman of the State Board of Charities. When the day arrived, Annie followed the group of men on their tour, with no one taking any notice of her. Just as Sanborn was preparing to leave, Annie burst from the crowd and threw herself at the blurry figures, not knowing which one was Sanborn and not able to see well enough anyway. "Mr. Sanborn!" she cried. "I want to go to school!"

Mr. Sanborn asked Annie what was wrong with her eyes and how long had she been at the poorhouse. Soon after they left, Annie was told to pack her meager belongings. She was being sent to school at the Perkins Institution.

Annie at the Perkins Institution

Annie was going to school, but it certainly was not easy for her. Most of the students at Perkins were well-off, and poverty-stricken Annie stuck out terribly. She had never worn a nightgown. She did not own a comb. She knew that her clothes, two dresses given to her before she left Tewksbury, were cheap and ugly. Annie was terribly ashamed of her poverty and background. She was also very proud and angry and began rebelling against her teachers and the other students. She became known for her rude responses and regular disobedience.

The teachers could not just dismiss Annie as another problem student because everyone soon realized that Annie was one of the smartest students at the school. Once an operation restored much of Annie's vision, enabling her to read, her enormous appetite for learning only increased.

By the time Annie graduated from Perkins as **valedictorian** of her class in 1886, she was a different girl from the one who had entered from the Tewksbury poorhouse so many years ago—and yet she was exactly the same. She was still fiery, quick-tempered, and opinionated, but she had developed social manners, a taste for lovely clothes, and a greater understanding of the world. She was also twenty years old, desperately poor, and in need of a job.

This photograph shows the Perkins Institution as Annie Sullivan might have known it. Today, the school is called the Perkins School for the Blind and still provides education for blind and deaf-blind students.

Michael Anagnos, Annie's friend and mentor, knew that she was the perfect person for the Kellers' situation.

Annie's Arrival

Annie set out from Boston to Tuscumbia in early March 1887. The Kellers met her at the train station; "I tried with all my might to control the eagerness that made me tremble so that I could hardly walk," Annie wrote later.

Helen was waiting on the porch. The house had been in a flurry for days, Captain Keller told Annie, and Helen knew that something was going to happen. She could tell by the preparation of Annie's room and the comings and goings as the Kellers ran back and forth from the train station, not sure which train the new teacher was arriving on. As Annie mounted the steps, Helen felt the vibrations of her feet on the wood and rushed at her, almost knocking her over in her eagerness to greet the visitor.

She was dirty, Annie observed, and unkempt, but her body was healthy and sturdy and her face attractive, though there was a strange emptiness in her expression. Once inside the house, Helen immediately tried to open Annie's bag, expecting treats; and when her mother restrained her, she threw a tantrum, giving Annie a brief glimpse of what would follow in the days ahead. However, Annie was made of stern stuff. She distracted Helen by placing a little watch in her hands and letting her feel the vibrations of the ticking and the smooth watchcase. The next morning, Annie opened her bag and gave Helen a doll sent by some of the girls at Perkins and dressed in beautiful clothes by Laura Bridgman herself.

Then Annie got right to work on the manual alphabet. She took Helen's hand and spelled *doll* into it. Helen, confused, threw

In this nineteenth-century photograph from the Perkins School archives, Helen and Annie are shown seated in a garden. In her lap, Helen holds a doll similar to the one Annie brought her from Perkins.

the doll to the floor. Annie ran downstairs and got a piece of cake from the kitchen. She brought it up and spelled the word *cake* to Helen. Helen did make the finger movements back this time, but she did not understand what she was doing. She simply imitated the movements and was rewarded with the cake, which she stuffed in her mouth all at once.

Disciplining Helen

Over the next few days, Annie got to know her new pupil a little better. She could see that she would get nowhere without correcting Helen's manners. "The greatest problem I shall have to solve is how to discipline and control her without breaking her spirit," Annie wrote in a letter back to Perkins. "I shall not attempt to conquer her by force alone; but I shall insist on reasonable obedience from the start." Soon after Annie's arrival, she got the chance to put her words into action.

At breakfast one morning, Helen started her usual round of the table, roaming around the room and taking whatever she wanted from other people's plates. Annie refused to let Helen eat from her plate. Helen immediately started kicking and raging. Annie could see that it was important that she not back down. So she asked the Keller family to leave the room and locked the door after them. Unaware that the family had left the room, Helen threw herself under the table where Annie was calmly continuing her breakfast. Helen kicked at Annie and tried to yank her chair out from under her.

Her teacher ignored her until Helen gave Annie a vicious pinch. Then Annie grabbed Helen and slapped her. For the first time, Helen had met someone who would fight back. She must have been very surprised. The two tussled for a while before Annie prevailed. Once Helen realized she had been left alone with this terrible intruder, she sat

"I shall not attempt to conquer her by force alone; but I shall insist on reasonable obedience from the start."

down at her own place, but began to eat with her fingers. Annie insisted she use a spoon and forced it into her hand. Helen immediately pitched the spoon onto the floor. Over and over they fought, until finally Helen yielded and finished her breakfast with her spoon. Then the two fought an hour-long battle when

Helen refused to fold her napkin. Finally, Helen folded the napkin. Annie unlocked the door and ran upstairs to her room, where she threw herself on her bed and cried—possibly out of sheer exhaustion and stress. It was almost lunchtime.

Moving to the Annex

Part of Helen's behavior problem was her parents. The Kellers could not deny Helen anything; and even though her rages were awful, the Captain and Kate could not stand seeing their daughter disciplined. Annie realized that Helen's behavior would never be curbed as long as she remained near her parents. Also, Helen

Helen and Annie lived in this two-room annex near the main house at Ivy Green early on in Helen's education. This contemporary photograph shows the annex as it looks today.

needed to feel more dependent on Annie so that she would have the desire to listen to her. Annie had to take Helen away somewhere, just the two of them. Luckily, the perfect place was right at Ivy Green.

Set only forty feet from the main house was a little cottage with one large room and one small room. The Kellers had lived there briefly after they were married, and Helen had been born there. Annie told the Kellers that she needed to take Helen away to the cottage alone for a while—just the two of them with no interference. The Kellers were reluctant but agreed that some drastic measures needed to be taken if Helen were going to improve.

The cottage was cleaned and the furniture rearranged so that it would be unfamiliar to Helen. Then, so that she would not know where she was, the Captain took Helen for a long, circuitous carriage ride before bringing her to the cottage. Once Helen found herself with only Annie and not knowing she was only yards from her house, Helen was frightened and enraged. She threw tantrum after tantrum; but this time, there were no sympathetic parents to soothe her tears, only patient and unemotional Annie who merely waited for her to stop. For the first couple of days, Helen would stand near the door and pat her cheek, the sign for her mother, over and over. Annie, however, remained firm. Helen must learn that she, Annie, was in charge now.

CHAPTER 3

Learning the World

A miracle has happened! The light of understanding has shown upon my little pupil's mind, and behold, all things are changed!

—Annie Sullivan

Helen's **guttural** screams and crashings were easily heard from the open windows of the main house, and the Kellers were concerned. What was going on over there? One morning, the Captain peeked in the window and saw Helen still in her nightgown at ten o'clock with her breakfast uneaten on the table. Apparently, Annie would not let her eat breakfast until she got dressed. Filled with worry, the Captain raged to his wife that no daughter of his would be deprived of food. He threatened to send Annie home.

Still, Annie must have sensed that her methods would work because she did not let up. And on March 20, just over two weeks after Annie's arrival, while they were still living in the annex, Annie wrote in a letter, "My heart is singing for joy this morning. A miracle has happened! The light of understanding has shown upon my little pupil's mind, and behold, all things are changed! The wild little creature of two weeks ago has been transformed into a gentle child." Helen let Annie kiss her now and sat beside her, crocheting and doing beadwork.

Just what was this "miracle"? Annie never says specifically, but perhaps Helen finally realized that Annie

In this photograph, Annie is spelling into Helen's hand while Helen is concentrating on her teacher's finger movements.

could teach her many wonderful things if she would only pay attention. Perhaps Annie's stronger will simply conquered Helen's, and Helen decided it was easier to love than to fight. One of Helen's biographers suggests that Annie found a way of cutting off Helen's growing source of communication—her hands—perhaps by tying them and refusing to spell to Helen when she misbehaved. Helen alluded to this later in her writing, though it is not known if Annie used or discovered this method during the days in the annex.

Now that Helen's behavior was under control, both Annie and Helen could turn their attention to the true task: learning language. Helen already knew many different words and could spell them to Annie and understand when they were spelled to her. However, she mixed up words a lot. For instance, Helen knew that the words *mug* and *milk* meant something to drink, but she would make a pouring motion when she spelled *mug*, and she would spell *milk* when pointing to the mug. Annie wrote in a letter that "[Helen] has no idea yet that everything has a name." In other words, Helen did not understand the greater purpose of language—that words could be used to communicate all sorts of thoughts—from identifying a simple object, such as a cup, to expressing a feeling or action, such as thirst or drinking. All of that would soon change, though.

The Awakening

By early April in 1887, Annie and Helen returned to the main house and were still wrestling with language problems. Then, one morning on the fifth of April, while washing up Helen indicated to Annie that she wanted to know what this cool, wet liquid was that flowed over her hands. Annie spelled W-A-T-E-R into Helen's hand, but it was obvious to Annie that a key connection was still missing from Helen's mind. She still did not understand that the manual language gestures Annie was constantly performing in Helen's hands had a meaning—and the specific hand movements Annie was now using on her pupil's palm meant *water*. To Helen, those hand gestures had no purpose. They were just finger games to mimic and copy back to Annie.

Then an idea occurred to Annie. Maybe Helen's desire to know the name for water could help Helen. The pair went out into the bright southern sunshine, and Helen skipped ahead of

The Manual Alphabet

The manual finger alphabet was first invented by monks in Spain, who would spell to one another so as not to break their vows of silence. By the early eighteenth century, French people were using the manual alphabet as a way of communicating with deaf people.

Each letter in the manual alphabet is represented by a sign. The sign for A, for instance, has the fingers folded down on the palm with the thumb sticking up. The typical manual alphabet is for people who are deaf but not blind. The deaf-blind manual alphabet is a little different. The letter signs are modified somewhat, and each is spelled into the open palm of the listener. The sign for A in the deaf-blind alphabet is made by touching the tip of the listener's thumb.

This poster from the American Foundation for the Blind shows Helen's own hands forming the letters of the manual alphabet.

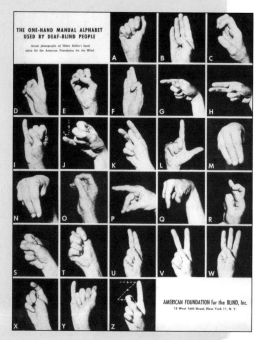

THE ONE-HAND MANUAL ALPHABET USED BY DEAF-BLIND PEOPLE

Actual photographs of Helen Keller's hand taken for the American Foundation for the Blind.

AMERICAN FOUNDATION for the BLIND, Inc.
15 West 16th Street, New York 11, N. Y.

Annie to the pump house—where the water pump was kept. There, Annie had Helen hold her cup under the water while Annie pumped and at the same time spelled *water* into Helen's hand. More pumping and then, *water* again. Something about the cold water flowing over her hand and the spelling at the same time turned on a switch in Helen's mind. She *got* it. As Annie wrote later, "She has learned that *everything has a name, and that the manual alphabet is the key to everything she wants to know.*"

She still did not understand that the manual language gestures Annie was constantly performing in Helen's hands had a meaning . . .

Helen's face was filled with wonder and joy. She spelled *water* to Annie several times, and then started asking for names of other objects—the ground, a trellis, the pump, and then she touched Annie and motioned. Annie spelled *teacher*. At last, Helen understood that Annie had a name, too. All the way back to the house, Helen asked Annie to name objects, reveling in her new world. Within a few hours, Helen added thirty new words to her vocabulary.

Many historians believe that morning at the pump marked the emergence of Helen's personality. Helen was naturally bright and, for most of her previous life, was inexpressibly angry at not being able to communicate. Annie opened the door and gave Helen the ability to express herself through language, revealing Helen's curious, delightful nature.

After the morning at the pump, Helen progressed incredibly fast. She was so busy absorbing knowledge she did not have time to misbehave. Soon she was learning not only nouns, but also verbs, adjectives, abstract thoughts, and simple sentences. Of course, Helen's personality was not *completely* transformed. She

Helen finally understood the greater purpose of language at the water pump at Ivy Green, shown here in this photograph.

was still willful and could occasionally lapse into her old behavior. Now, though, Helen understood that her actions had consequences. When Helen bit and scratched Viney, the little daughter of one of the Kellers' servants, Annie communicated to Helen that she was very sad at her behavior. Helen was very upset, and after a whole day of sadness, she went to Viney and apologized by letting Viney kiss her.

Living and Learning

Helen hardly realized she was doing work. In fact, because of Annie's style of teaching, Helen thought that learning was the most fun thing she had ever done. Annie was a self-taught teacher—no one had told her that there was a certain way to teach or for students to learn. She just taught Helen in the way she thought best.

One day, Helen's little cousin came to visit the Kellers with her parents. Annie watched the way the adults interacted with the fifteen-month-old, who was just learning language. People spoke to the child in full sentences, using figures of speech, abstract thoughts, and adjectives even though the child could not understand everything that was being said to her. Annie realized the child would eventually simply absorb the rhythms and patterns of speech naturally and would figure out the meanings of different words and parts of speech partly by herself. She decided to employ the same method with Helen.

Every day, all day long, Annie used the manual alphabet to convey ordinary language to Helen, whether or not Helen could understand everything she was trying to communicate. Annie and Helen studied and learned all through the hot Alabama summer. The pair would leave the main house and roam the fields of Ivy Green, the river, and the barnyard. They would climb trees and examine rocks, flowers, and insects, and all the time Annie would pour conversation, explanation, and description into Helen's hand.

The method worked. Helen was entranced. Annie could not spell fast enough to keep up with Helen's questions. Helen wanted to communicate and learn all day, as if she were making up for all the time lost. At night, Helen would spell in her sleep.

By June 1887, Helen knew four hundred words. Annie wrote that she had been transformed from a wild child to one who insisted on having her hair put in curl papers every night. Annie taught Helen to read Braille, the raised-dot system for blind people,

Helen and Annie spent many days and weeks exploring the grounds of Ivy Green. This photograph shows those grounds as they look today.

and Helen began devouring books, as she would for the rest of her life. Soon Helen was reading poems by popular American poets Henry Wadsworth Longfellow and Oliver Wendell Holmes.

The Kellers were excited by Helen's progress and eager to spell to her. However, Annie was very possessive of her charge— a pattern that would continue for the rest of Annie's own life. For instance, she would not permit Kate to hire a nurse to help care for Helen, telling Kate that she wanted no one interfering with her interactions with Helen. Annie even resented Kate's attempts to learn the manual alphabet and talk to her daughter. She told Kate that she, Annie, was to be the only one to teach Helen words.

Annie may not have been perfect, but she had transformed not only Helen's life, but also that of the entire Keller family. Christmas 1887 was a reverent and thankful time. Annie wrote,

Braille

Braille is a system by which blind people can read using their fingers. Before Braille, the few books that were printed for the blind used raised regular alphabet letters. These letters were hard for readers to feel, and the books had to be very big to accommodate the larger-sized letters. With the Braille system, a series of raised dots on a page represents words, punctuation, and numbers. The reader slides his or her fingers across the page, feeling the dots with the fingertips. Experienced Braille readers can read around one or two hundred words a minute, about the same as a sighted person reading printed words.

This photograph depicts a page of Braille words. A person reads Braille by trailing his or her fingers lightly across the dots.

Braille was invented in 1824 by a young blind man named Louis Braille. Louis was attending the Royal Institute for Blind Youth in Paris when he met a former soldier in Napoleon's army. This soldier had with him a system of raised-dot reading he had invented so that the army could read documents at night without a light. He called it "night writing." However, the system was way too complicated and the soldiers never wound up using it. Louis simplified the system and in 1829, at the age of twenty, Louis published the first Braille book.

This statue of Louis Braille, the inventor of the Braille system, stands in Buenos Aires, Argentina.

These words were written by Helen in June 1887. Even though some of the round letters look square, all of her writing is readable.

"It was evident that every one, especially Captain and Mrs. Keller, was deeply moved at the thought of the difference between this bright Christmas and the last. . . . As we came downstairs, Mrs. Keller said to me with tears in her eyes, 'Miss Annie, I thank God every day of my life for sending you to us; but I never realized until this morning what a blessing you have been to us.'" For Helen, life would never be the same.

CHAPTER 4

Fame and Heartbreak

The winter of 1892 was darkened by the one cloud in my childhood's bright sky. . . . A little story called "The Frost King" . . . was at the root of the trouble.

Since her arrival in Tuscumbia, Annie had been writing regular reports of Helen's progress to Michael Anagnos, the director of the Perkins Institution. The director was thrilled with Helen's progress—for here was an example of what could be achieved with deaf-blind students. In 1888, Anagnos placed in the annual report for the school a lengthy account of Helen, Annie, and their miraculous progress. His flowery, florid descriptions of Helen were captivating, and soon the mainstream press became interested in the story.

The public was already familiar with Laura Bridgman and the story of her education, so when word spread of the new deaf-blind **prodigy** in Alabama, people seized on the story.

Some of the news reports were greatly exaggerated and even blatantly untrue. For instance, there were accounts that Helen could play the piano brilliantly, recognize colors by touch, and speak seven languages. Annie was dismayed by the exaggerations. She reminded everyone whenever she could that Helen was just an ordinary little girl and that she still had a long way to go in her education.

Nonetheless, the public was fascinated by Helen. Every day, she received letters from people who marveled at her accomplishments. Helen did not mind a bit—in fact, she reveled in the attention. She was making up for all the years stuck in isolation and loved communicating with her admirers.

Helen quickly began using her newfound fame to advocate for others. Through letters to **patrons**, she raised money for a deaf-blind boy named Tommy Stringer, who was poor and uneducated. With Helen's help, Tommy was eventually sent to kindergarten for blind children at Perkins. In fact, after Helen's dog was accidentally shot by a policeman and people sent her money to help buy a new dog, she instead asked for donations to help fund Tommy's education.

Helen poses with other Perkins students in this undated photograph. Helen stands at the top left while Tommy Stringer, whose education she helped fund, sits at the bottom right.

This 1891 photograph shows an eleven-year-old Helen in profile, with her non-protruding eye toward the camera and her chestnut curls carefully styled.

By now, Helen was being photographed regularly by the press, so Annie made sure she was always fashionably dressed in beautiful clothes and immaculately groomed, with her chestnut curls beautifully displayed. Since Helen's left eye, which was obviously blind, protruded noticeably, Annie made sure her pupil was exclusively photographed in right profile.

The World Beyond Tuscumbia

Helen's world soon expanded beyond Tuscumbia. In May 1888, Helen, Annie, and Kate Keller set out to visit the Perkins Institution at the invitation of Michael Anagnos. This would be the first time in her life that Helen would meet other blind children.

In this photograph from 1894, an adolescent Helen, her good friend Alexander Graham Bell, and Annie gather at the meeting for the American Association to Promote the Teaching of Speech to the Deaf in Chautauqua, New York.

The trio set out for Massachusetts by train, but first they made a stop in Washington, D.C., where Helen visited with her good friend Alexander Graham Bell. Ever since their first meeting and Helen's breakthrough, Bell and Helen had kept up a regular correspondence. Helen felt very close to the old, white-bearded man, who she regarded as a friend and a grandfather figure.

Helen was even invited to the White House by President Grover Cleveland. In Boston, Helen attended the Perkins school commencement and dazzled the crowd with her and Annie's demonstration of the manual finger alphabet. Then they traveled to Cape Cod to spend time with Annie's housemother from her own days at Perkins, Mrs. Hopkins. While at the cape, Helen experienced for the first time the joy of being tumbled in the ocean waves, a memory she wrote about later: "The buoyant motion of the water filled me with an exquisite, quivering joy. Suddenly my ecstasy gave place to terror; for my foot struck against a rock and the next instant there was a rush of water over my head. I thrust out my hands to grasp at some support, I clutched at the water and at the seaweed which the waves tossed in my face. . . . At last, however, the sea, as if weary of its new toy, threw me back on the shore. . . . As soon as I had recovered from my panic sufficiently to say anything, I demanded: 'Who put salt in the water?' "

In the fall of 1889, Helen and Annie traveled again to Perkins. This time, Helen stayed several months as the guest of the school. She took lessons and started studying French, amazing her teachers with her wit and remarkable memory.

Learning to Speak

Helen loved learning and studying, and in March 1890 she developed a new obsession—learning to speak. A former teacher at Perkins returning from abroad told Helen about a deaf-blind girl in Norway who had been taught to speak. This news lit a fire in Helen, who constantly craved communication with the world. Of course, she could communicate now by using the manual alphabet, but she was limited in doing so with those who knew the system—and only a few hearing-sighted people did. If she could speak, Helen could then talk with whomever she wanted!

As much as Helen wanted to speak, she didn't know *how* to do it—that is, to form words with the movement of her lips and tongue and to combine them with sound from her voice box. With her characteristic determination, Helen begged Annie to find her a voice teacher. At first, Annie was reluctant—she found the often-distorted voices of deaf people unpleasant. Helen persisted, and eventually Annie relented. Sarah Fuller, principal of a school for the deaf in Boston, agreed to take Helen on as a pupil and began lessons immediately. Miss Fuller let Helen feel the position and movement of her tongue and lips when she made a distinct

This print shows Sarah Fuller, the teacher who first taught Helen to lip-read.

noise, such as *m*. Within one hour in the first lesson, Helen had learned to make six letter sounds.

At home, Helen and Annie would practice her voice lessons. Helen had to put her entire hand into Annie's mouth as she spoke to feel the placement of her lips and tongue. Sometimes, she put her fingers so far back in Annie's throat that she accidentally made her teacher gag.

Helen also learned to "lip-read" by placing a middle finger on the speaker's nose to feel the exhalations of air, an index finger on the lips to feel the movement, and a thumb on the throat so she could feel the vibrations of speech. In this way, she could understand normal conversation.

Helen had made a good start in learning about oral speech, and she assumed that she would soon be speaking normally. She sometimes made herself sick from anxiety and exhaustion practicing her voice lessons. However, what neither Helen nor

In this 1897 photograph, Helen reads Annie's lips by placing her fingers on her teacher's throat, mouth, and nose.

Annie realized was that Sarah Fuller's method of teaching was flawed. Helen would never speak normally with these methods because her voice box was underdeveloped and needed to be exercised before she could make distinct sounds. She should have been studying with a singing teacher, for instance, learning how to make noise before trying to say words.

Even though Helen did eventually learn to speak, her speech would never be fully understood. Her words were slurred, and

Oral Speech vs. Sign Language

Helen Keller came of age during an important debate about the proper education of deaf people. The manual alphabet, in which deaf people indicated their words through finger and hand movements, was widespread by the time Helen was a child, yet the Kellers followed the advice of their friend Alexander Graham Bell, who was a strong advocate of oralism, or oral speech. Bell advocated that deaf people should be taught to lip-read and speak—in other words, to mimic as closely as possible the communication of their hearing peers, rather than use sign language. Helen had to use the manual alphabet, of course, but at Perkins, this was used only as a tool to move her toward lip-reading and speech—the "best" forms of communication.

This photograph shows a young student learning the manual alphabet with her teacher, c. 1890.

she had trouble with certain letters. Moreover, her voice had a distinct tinny, metallic sound, and she spoke in a monotone. Throughout her long life and many public appearances, Helen would almost always need to speak through an interpreter. She would speak aloud, and someone who understood her voice—usually Annie—would repeat Helen's words for the audience.

For now, Helen was working hard, learning, and loving her life that had been so completely transformed over the last four years. The world, she felt, loved her, and she loved the world. Helen was soon forced to recognize a difficult truth: The world was not always wonderful and forgiving.

"The Frost King"

On November 4, 1891, when she was eleven, Helen mailed Michael Anagnos a story she had written for his birthday. She called her little fairy tale "The Frost King"—a fable about a ruler who reigned over a land of endless snow.

Anagnos loved the story. He arranged to have it reproduced in the Perkins alumni magazine as well as another magazine for deaf and blind people. Before too long, though, Anagnos heard that Helen's little tale was almost

Helen poses with Michael Anagnos in this photograph from the Perkins School History Museum. Anagnos was a great admirer of Helen before "The Frost King" episode.

identical to a story written by author Margaret T. Canby, titled "The Frost Fairies."

Anagnos was upset and embarrassed. He was forced to print a humiliating retraction of the story. What had happened? Had Helen copied Canby's story? Anagnos decided that the matter must be investigated and wrote immediately to Annie. When Annie told Helen that Anagnos thought her story was not her own and suspected her of **plagiarism**, Helen was devastated. Her words not her own? She would never steal anyone else's thoughts. Helen wracked her brain but could not remember having knowledge of Canby's story. Finally, Annie and she concluded that one summer on Cape Cod, Mrs. Hopkins must have related the story to Helen, and Helen, having forgotten she had experienced it, may have retained it in the depths of her mind somewhere. Helen's impressive memory was well-known, so this was a likely scenario. Later, some historians speculated that Annie herself had read Helen the story and was too embarrassed at the time to admit it. Instead, she concocted a lie and convinced Helen of it.

Brought Before a Court

The miserable episode was far from over. Anagnos, thoroughly humiliated, turned against Helen and decided that the plagiarism charge should be examined before a court of eight Perkins teachers and officials. Meanwhile, letters of encouragement came in from several of Helen's supporters. Even Margaret Canby wrote a gracious letter to Helen, forgiving her. Nonetheless, Anagnos was determined that the matter should be settled once and for all. Perhaps he also had a secret wish to see Helen put on the spot as he felt *he* had been.

At the examination, Helen was not allowed to have Annie or her mother with her as she was questioned by the four blind and four hearing-sighted officials. Instead, Annie had to wait in the hall outside. Through a substitute translator, Helen was asked how she wrote the story, where she heard it, how she could remember the story

Anagnos, thoroughly humiliated, turned against Helen and decided that the plagiarism charge should be examined . . .

having heard it so long ago. At the end, the faculty voted on whether to believe Helen's claims of innocence. The decision was split 4–4, until Anagnos, in a surprising move, cast the deciding vote in favor of Helen.

After the incident was over, Helen and Annie retreated to Tuscumbia. As far as Anagnos and the Perkins school were concerned, the matter was finished, but Helen was deeply scarred by the incident. The trauma of having a person she thought was a friend accuse her of a crime was upsetting enough, but just as distressing was the psychological torture of not being able to remember copying the text. "I have ever since been tortured by the fear that what I write is not my own," Helen wrote many years later.

Anxious and depressed, Helen had no confidence in herself. When writing letters, even to her mother, she would often stop to ask Annie if the writing was indeed her own. Finally, Annie arranged for Helen to write a biography of her life thus far for the children's magazine *Youth's Companion*. The article was published and slowly, slowly Helen began to regain a fragile confidence. For the rest of her life, however, she would never forget "The Frost King" episode.

Helen's Favorite Books

From the time she learned Braille until the end of her life, Helen remained a voracious reader. When she was only a child, Annie read to her from Homer's *Iliad* and *Odyssey* by spelling the words of the books into Helen's hand using the manual alphabet. Later, Helen read in Braille Shakespeare's plays and the Bible, as well as works by the popular poets Oliver Wendell Holmes and Henry Wadsworth Longfellow. One of Helen's true loves, though, was fairy tales. She devoured the Brothers Grimm, Hans Christian Andersen, and *The Arabian Nights*. Annie insisted that Helen read quality literature, but Helen did not always obey. Once, when Annie caught Helen reading the modern, popular novel *The Last Days of Pompeii* that had been translated into Braille, she was furious and spelled angrily to Helen that she had discovered and trapped her.

This statue in Germany shows the Brothers Grimm, whose fairy tales Helen Keller greatly enjoyed reading in Braille.

CHAPTER 5

Helen in the Big City

People . . . have expressed surprise that I should notice any difference . . . between walking in city streets and in country roads. They forget that my whole body is alive to the conditions about me.

Though she could not see or hear, Helen was not trapped in a box of dark silence. In addition to her sensitive sense of touch, Helen relied heavily on vibration and smell to offer information about the world. Helen was so sensitive to vibrations that she could feel a pencil falling off a desk to the floor. She could identify a person in the house just from the vibrations of his or her footfalls in a room beneath the room she was sitting in. She could even feel the vibrations of passing airplanes when she was inside.

Helen learned to enjoy music also. Sometimes, musicians would perform for Helen personally. She would hold the end of a violin and "listen" to the music by sensing the vibrations coming through the instrument. In this same way, she appreciated opera. By placing one hand in the lip-reading position and the other on the singer's chest, Helen could sense the musical tones through the vibrations she felt.

Helen's sense of smell was also unusually developed. She could smell a storm approaching or could tell what sort of a house she was in by the smell—whether an older house or a newer one—and what kind of activities went on

By placing her hands on a musical instrument to feel the vibrations, Helen could enjoy music. In this c. 1904 photograph, she touches the piano as the musician plays.

in that house—cooking, perhaps, or ironing, or laundry. She could also sense peoples' occupations by the scents they carried on their clothes and persons; doctors, carpenters, and gardeners all smelled different to Helen. Helen could even tell where people had been just before they came to see her by smelling them.

Setting a High Goal

These senses and years of practice helped Helen navigate her world. Yet simply existing in the world was not enough for Helen—she wanted to *know* the world, too. When she was a little girl, Helen declared to Annie, her family, and anyone else who would pay attention that not only did she intend to be educated, but she was also going to go to college.

Helen's Sense of Touch

In this excerpt from Helen's book *The World I Live In*, she describes the importance of the world of touch:

"My world is built of touch-sensations, devoid of physical color and sound; but without color and sound it breathes and throbs with life. Every object is associated in my mind with tactual [touchable] qualities which, combined in countless ways, give me a sense of power, of beauty, or of incongruity [humor]: for with my hands I can feel the comic as well as the beautiful in the outward appearance of things. Remember that you, dependent on your sight, do not realize how many things are tangible. All palpable things are mobile or rigid, solid or liquid, big or small, warm or cold, and these qualities are variously modified. The coolness of the water-lily rounding into bloom is different from the coolness of an evening wind in summer, and different again from the coolness of the rain that soaks into the hearts of growing things and gives them life and body. The velvet of the rose is not that of a ripe peach or of a baby's dimpled cheek. The hardness of the rock is to the hardness of wood what a man's deep bass is to a woman's voice when it is low. What I call beauty I find in certain combinations of all these qualities, and is largely derived from the flow of curved and straight lines which is over all things."

This was a very unusual declaration. No one had ever heard of a deaf-blind person attending college before. College was still seen as a school for upper-class men. Times were changing, though, and during the latter half of the nineteenth century,

The buildings of Radcliffe College are shown in this 1910 photograph.

college education for women had exploded in the United States. More and more, American women were demanding the chance to attend college, and schools were responding. By the 1890s, there were 217 women's colleges in the country and 465 coeducational schools.

Helen wanted the same thing so many American women of her time wanted. Never content to do halfway what she could do fully, Helen also declared that she had chosen the most prestigious women's college in the country as her goal: Radcliffe College, the women's counterpart to Harvard University.

Most likely, Helen's family and friends doubted she could ever master the advanced high-school lessons needed to pass the Radcliffe entrance exams. There was one person, however, who never underestimated Helen and who never doubted she could achieve the highest goals available to any person, deaf, hearing, blind, sighted, or otherwise—Annie. Annie was determined that if Helen wanted to go to college, she was going to do everything she could to help her get there.

Life in New York

College days were still far off and Helen had years of hard work ahead of her. First, she needed to both work on her speaking skills and begin a rigorous course of high school study. In fall 1894, Annie and Helen moved to New York so Helen could attend the Wright-Humason School for the Deaf. The founders of the Wright-Humason School had met Helen and believed their methods could improve her still-incomprehensible speaking voice.

Helen was fourteen when she and Annie made their way to New York. Although she had been to the White House and lived in Boston, it is easy to imagine the thrill that she must have felt in the city of New York. At the turn of the nineteenth century, the massive city was a belching, steaming stew of carriages, horses, coal wagons, train engines, baking bread, soot, smoke, fresh flowers, sewers, tenements, mansions, and slums. Helen loved it all. She reveled in the excitement and fast pace of the city, but one of her favorite activities was galloping her horse every morning in Central Park, the largest public park in Manhattan, beside Annie.

Radcliffe College

Radcliffe College was only an infant school of higher learning when Helen Keller set her sights on attending. Founded in 1894 as the women's counterpart to Harvard University, the requirements for women students were the same as those at Harvard, and classes were taught by Harvard professors. In its earliest days, the women squeezed into two rooms for their classes and used the bathroom as a lab for physics and chemistry experiments.

Change at Radcliffe began during World War II, when Harvard allowed women to attend classes at the university for the first time. Over the following decades, the two schools began to merge more and more, and by 1977 the schools had officially merged. Radcliffe was finally absorbed fully into Harvard in 1999.

Helen was not the only famous graduate of Radcliffe. Over the decades, movie stars, politicians, authors, and artists have graduated from the school. The late prime minister of Pakistan, Benazir Bhutto, graduated from Radcliffe, as did the Canadian author Margaret Atwood, the actress Stockard Channing, the writer Francine Prose, the poet Adrienne Rich, and the feminist writer and poet Gertrude Stein.

The 1902 graduating class of Radcliffe poses outside one of their buildings wearing their commencement caps and gowns.

Helen loved riding through Central Park with Annie during her time in New York. This photograph was taken c. 1907.

Helen was a bit of a celebrity in the city; she and Annie made many wealthy and powerful friends in the drawing rooms of New York's upper class. These relationships were essential to the pair, because for some time now Annie and Helen had depended on the charity of rich patrons in order to pay for their living expenses and Helen's education. The Keller family had less money than ever and could not support Helen's lifestyle. In fact, Captain Keller owed Annie years of wages he never paid. He even borrowed money from Helen on several occasions. Cultivating and maintaining friendships with patrons was an essential part of Helen's existence.

The oil baron John D. Rockefeller was one such patron, as was the wealthy writer Laurence Hutton, who later put together a fund for Helen's education. The sugar magnate John S. Spaulding supported Helen during his life and promised to provide an

This portrait depicts Samuel Clemens, also known as Mark Twain, as he looked when Helen knew him. The two remained close friends throughout Clemens's life.

inheritance for her in his will. One of Helen's dearest friends, whom she met during this period and to whom she remained very close until his death, was Samuel Clemens, the writer and satirist best known by his pseudonym, Mark Twain. The two appreciated each other's spirit and sharp wit, and Clemens was one of Helen's staunchest defenders. Throughout her life, whenever Helen visited Clemens at his home in Connecticut, he always made sure her room was stocked with whiskey and cigars—the essentials for any houseguest, he was sure.

Helen and Annie were popular and busy, but the Wright-Humason School was not turning out to be a success. Helen felt isolated from the other deaf students, who were sighted, and she had to take arithmetic, which she hated. Her struggles with math would plague her throughout her education. In addition, she was making very little progress with her speaking. Her voice was hardly intelligible to anyone who did not know her well, despite constant practice.

To add to the difficulties, in January 1896 John Spaulding died without leaving Helen the legacy he had promised, making no mention of it in his will. Helen and Annie had been counting on the money to help support them. Then on August 19, 1896,

In this photograph c. 1895, the first graduating class of the Wright-Humason school poses together. Helen is seated at the far left, turned in profile, and holding Annie's hand.

Helen's father, Captain Keller, died. He also left no money for Helen—only massive debt. Helen and Annie were in Massachusetts with friends when they heard of the Captain's death, but Kate Keller refused to allow Helen to come home for the funeral, feeling that the Alabama heat would be bad for Helen's health. Helen was left to grieve for her father alone and continue her worries about money. For now, she and Annie would have to depend on the generosity of their other benefactors.

Helen was able to take some comfort in her new religious beliefs. Around the time of the death of her father, Helen became interested in the religion of Swedenborgianism. This branch of Christianity is based on the writings of eighteenth-century philosopher Emanuel Swedenborg. Believers follow the principles

This formal portrait depicts Emanuel Swedenborg, the founder of Swedenborgianism—a religion that appealed to Helen.

that good originates in God, evil originates in humans, and the duty of all people is to do good acts and shun evil ones. Helen was no doubt also attracted by the promise of an afterlife in which all people would be whole and complete, without limitations.

Incident at the Cambridge School

When Helen was sixteen, it became obvious that she could not stay at the Wright-Humason School if she was to pass the Radcliffe entrance exams. She needed a more advanced education, and as usual she and Annie set their sights on one of the best college-prep schools for girls in Massachusetts called the Cambridge School for Young Ladies. The Cambridge School was a school for the typical hearing-sighted student, a first for Helen. However, she was unfazed and was accepted in October 1896— after some deliberation from the school director, Arthur Gilman. Later, the Kellers decided that Helen's younger sister, Mildred, would move from Tuscumbia to attend the school also. Even though the Kellers were not wealthy, they may have been able to send Mildred to the school because Helen's education was funded by her patrons.

Whatever concerns Mr. Gilman may have had about Helen were soon laid to rest. She did brilliantly at school the first year— so well that her course of study was shortened by an entire year. She especially distinguished herself in English. Annie attended

A teenage Helen and her sister, Mildred, are shown posing in white dresses in this 1897 photograph.

lectures with Helen and would spell the teachers' words into her hand. Helen would type her homework on her typewriter and would read from Braille books if she could get them, or Annie would read them to her into her hand.

Everything changed during Helen's second year. Her grades started going down drastically, mostly because she had to take a great deal of math, which was by far her worst subject. In addition, a printing delay in England made it difficult for Helen to get the Braille books she needed. Annie had to read and translate all the books for Helen, which was time-consuming and stressful for them both.

Helen's grades dropped and Annie starting worrying that Helen's benefactors would lose interest in her education if her performance were anything but stellar. She started pushing Helen to study harder, which was stressful for Helen and made her anxious. Helen became ill one month and spent a little time in bed, though it does not seem that her illness was related to stress.

Still, something about the combination of Annie's determination, Helen's anxiety, and her period of mild illness seemed to have convinced Arthur Gilman that Annie Sullivan was pushing Helen to study too hard—and toward a nervous breakdown. Mr. Gilman took a personal interest in this matter and took it upon himself to write letter after letter to Kate Keller, far away in Alabama, telling her that Annie was a dangerous influence on Helen. The two should be separated, in his opinion.

Annie attended lectures with Helen and would spell the teachers' words into her hand.

Kate was understandably alarmed, especially because she was not at the school to actually see what was going on. Mr. Gilman convinced Kate that Annie was abusing Helen. By telegram, Kate gave Mr. Gilman authorization to act as Helen's guardian to keep her safe. For Mr. Gilman, this meant removing Helen from Annie's care to his own. It is not entirely clear why Arthur Gilman behaved in such an extreme manner during this episode. Did he imagine that Helen had wealth he wished to obtain for himself? Was he eager to have control over her fame and celebrity? Did he genuinely believe that Helen was in danger of being drastically overworked?

Whatever the reasons, the incident was terribly upsetting for the pair. Annie was furious, of course, when she found out about Mr. Gilman's plans and threatened to remove both Helen and her sister from the school immediately, disregarding the fact that legally, Gilman was now Helen's guardian.

For her part, when Helen learned that she and Annie were to be separated, she became hysterical, weeping and refusing to eat or sleep. The strange affair was finally settled when Kate, after arriving in Massachusetts to examine the situation for herself, executed an astounding about-face, rescinded Mr. Gilman's guardianship, restored Annie to her position, and accused Mr. Gilman of abusing Kate's own authority. Annie and Helen were united again and ready for their next challenge—Radcliffe!

Helen's devotion to Annie is evident in this undated photograph, in which Helen rests her head on Annie's shoulder.

CHAPTER 6

A College Coed

I soon discovered that college was not quite the romantic lyceum I had imagined.

After the Gilman episode, Helen could not continue her studies at the Cambridge School. A private tutor helped her complete her courses. Helen passed the Radcliffe exams, and in fall 1900 became the first deaf-blind college student in the nation.

College was different from what Helen had expected. Since she was a young teenager, Helen had pictured the college experience as one of continuous intellectual inquiry, stimulating discussion, and constant exploration of new ideas. Radcliffe *was* a tremendously stimulating place to learn. However, Helen found herself feeling isolated from the rest of the students, who were all hearing and sighted. "I soon discovered that college was not quite the romantic **lyceum** I had imagined," Helen later wrote. "Many of the dreams that had delighted my young inexperience . . . 'faded into the

RADCLIFFE COLLEGE.

CERTIFICATE OF ADMISSION.

CAMBRIDGE, *July 28* 1899

Helen Adams Keller

is admitted to the Freshman Class in Radcliffe College.

Agnes Irwin
Dean of Radcliffe College.

Miss Keller passed with credit in Advanced Latin.

Helen's certificate of admission to Radcliffe College is shown here, signed by the Dean and noting that Helen is being admitted with credit in Advanced Latin.

light of common day.' " Though the women of Radcliffe were friendly to Helen, only one other student knew the manual alphabet. Even with Annie at her side to interpret, Helen found participating in conversations difficult.

A Difficult Adjustment

In addition to her troubles with isolation, Helen also found the college work far more difficult than anything she had encountered either with her private tutor or at the Cambridge School. Annie, who had only a high school education, was also struggling, unsure of the meanings of what she had to communicate to Helen. Nonetheless, the two continued with the system they had developed over the years: Annie attended every lecture with Helen and sat beside her, spelling into her hand the professor's words.

Helen could not take notes in class because her hands were occupied interpreting Annie's lecture details, so as soon as a class was over, she would retreat to her room to write down everything she remembered. Helen had a Braille typewriter on which to type her class notes, but assignments for her teachers had to be typed on a regular typewriter, so she could not go back to read what she had written. She was able to do some of her assigned reading in Braille or raised-type books. Frequently, though, the books Helen needed were not available in Braille. In those cases, Annie had to read to Helen in her hand, which was a tedious process.

Meanwhile, Annie was exhausted from the strain of spelling difficult material to Helen for hours every day. Annie's eyes, always bad, were growing worse from the constant reading. Helen could tell her teacher was tired. Often, when Annie asked if she wanted a passage reread, Helen would say no even if she did.

In this photograph from 1907, Helen reads from one of her many Braille books. She spent many hours reading to herself and being read to during her time at Radcliffe.

Exams were another hurdle to cross. The school was suspicious of Annie's interaction with Helen—how was anyone to know if Annie were just doing the work? So Annie was not allowed to be in the room at all. In fact, she had to leave the *building* when the exam began. A woman from the Perkins Institution was brought in to type out the exam questions in Braille. Helen could then read the questions and type out her answers on a typewriter that was provided. To oversee this unorthodox test taking, the dean of Radcliffe hired two proctors—people who watch over students taking an exam. The first proctor monitored Helen as she took the exams. The other watched the woman preparing the Braille questions.

To relieve some of her college stress, Helen would read about Swedenborgianism and play chess with Annie. She had an ingenious chessboard in which the white pieces were somewhat larger than the black so she could tell them apart, and the squares of the board had indentations for

The school was suspicious of Annie's interaction with Helen— how was anyone to know if Annie were just doing the work?

the pieces to rest in. She could tell by the faint vibration of the other player setting down his or her piece when it was her turn. Even when she was enjoying herself, Helen demonstrated her amazing mind: Without seeing the board like a sighted chess player, she kept the current positions of the pieces in her mind as she played.

In this photograph from about 1899, Helen and Annie play chess at Radcliffe. They are using Helen's specially designed chessboard.

A Reluctant Author

During Helen's second year at Radcliffe, she was invited by *Ladies' Home Journal* to write a series of articles about her life so far. Even though she was a college student, Helen was still famous, and the magazine editors obviously thought she would make a captivating author.

Helen accepted but soon found herself overwhelmed and confused by the work. Though she had done plenty of writing before, she had never written a connected series of pieces and had never attempted to tackle a work of such breadth. When she showed the pieces to the editors at *Ladies' Home Journal*, they were shocked at the poor quality of the writing—the articles were confusing, unstructured, and disorganized. In addition, Helen found that she disliked writing such long pieces and producing so much text. The task of writing was a burden, she thought. This was a feeling that would continue throughout Helen's life, though she would eventually write more than a dozen books.

Helen needed help with her articles, and help arrived in the form of John Albert Macy, who was introduced to Helen and Annie by a mutual friend. John Macy was quite a figure: twenty-five and a teacher of English at Harvard as well as an editor at the popular children's magazine *Youth's Companion*. He was tall, witty, handsome, and widely known as a brilliant writer and editor. John was just what Helen needed—an editor to help whip her articles into shape.

John, who had extensive knowledge of the publishing world, realized that Helen could easily compile the *Journal* articles into a book—one that would most likely be quite successful. Together, John, Annie, and Helen edited the articles into a memoir—or personal account—titled *The Story of My Life*. Then John, now functioning as a literary agent, successfully negotiated the best

The Story of My Life

BY
HELEN KELLER

WITH
HER LETTERS (1887—1901) AND A
SUPPLEMENTARY ACCOUNT OF
HER EDUCATION, INCLUDING
PASSAGES FROM THE REPORTS
AND LETTERS OF HER TEACHER,
ANNE MANSFIELD SULLIVAN
BY
JOHN ALBERT MACY

This is the title page from Helen's first memoir, *The Story of My Life*. John Macy is given credit as well.

contract with Doubleday for the publication, from among several competing publishers. *The Story of My Life* was published in March 1903 by Doubleday. Helen was twenty-two.

The book, however, was not the runaway best seller John had anticipated. It sold only ten thousand copies, or possibly fewer, in the first two years. Critics questioned Helen's use of visual and auditory imagery. How could she write of greens and whites, and light and dark, when she had no conception of those things? Helen explained that she used this language because it was part of the "normal" way of writing and though she did not know what "green" looked like, the colors and sounds represented feelings and sensations for her.

Affairs of the Heart

On June 28, 1904, Helen graduated from Radcliffe with honors. She was the first deaf-blind person ever to earn a bachelor of arts degree. Though Annie was upset that Helen had not earned a degree *summa cum laude*—meaning with highest honors—graduation was nonetheless a moment of great triumph and joy for Helen.

Even after Helen was finished with her memoir and had left college, John Macy remained in Annie and Helen's lives as their close friend. After all the long hours spent over the typewriter, spelling to Helen and discussing their plans for the future, it seemed natural that John should fall in love—but not with Helen, though she was just his age. No, John fell in love with Annie, who was in her late thirties, sickly, and growing quite stout as she neared middle age. Perhaps John was attracted to Annie's keen intellect—one that matched his own.

Helen poses in her cap and gown for this photograph at the time of her graduation from Radcliffe in 1904. She was the first deaf-blind person in history to graduate from college.

John was an ardent suitor—he wrote Annie passionate love letters and begged her over and over to marry him. For reasons that still are not entirely clear, Annie kept refusing John's proposals. She might have thought that it was only proper that a lady should refuse a gentleman's proposals several times before accepting. Maybe she was concerned about marrying someone several years younger than she. Or, she may have been worried about what would happen to Helen should she marry.

A c. 1900 portrait of John Macy as he might have appeared when he first met Annie and Helen. Although much younger, he fell in love with Annie Sullivan.

Perhaps to resolve her own conflicting feelings, Annie told John to ask Helen for her blessing—much in the same way a prospective suitor would ask the bride's father for permission. Helen insisted that Annie marry and be happy. Helen could not bear the thought that she might somehow be in the way of Annie's happiness. "She had devoted the best years of her womanhood to me," Helen wrote in her memoir *Midstream*, "and I had often longed to see her blessed with a good man's love." John just as graciously assured Helen that their marriage would be a marriage of three—much as if Helen were a beloved sister or grown child of Annie's. Helen would live with the Macys always and her relationship with Annie would continue unchanged.

Finally, Annie consented and the two were married on May 2, 1905, at the farmhouse in Wrentham, Massachusetts, which Annie and Helen had purchased together some years earlier. After Annie and John had a brief honeymoon in New Orleans—while Helen spent time with her mother in Tuscumbia—the three settled down in the Wrentham farmhouse to live what Helen would later remember as some of the happiest years of both her and Annie's lives.

Helen, Annie, and John pose with one of their dogs in this undated photograph at Wrentham.

CHAPTER 7

A Political and Social Activist

I want [the workers of the world] to have the same blessings that I have. . . . I want them to be helped as generously in a struggle which resembles my own in many ways.

The farmhouse at Wrentham perhaps reminded Helen a bit of Ivy Green, her childhood home. The large white-clapboard house sprawled on several acres, pleasantly shaded by large trees and surrounded by lush gardens. John had stretched ropes along a field so that

In this photograph c. 1910, the three-story house at Wrentham is draped in decorative American flags and bunting.

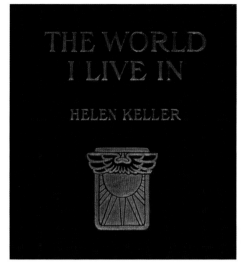

Shown here is the cover of Helen's book *The World I Live In*, in which she presents descriptions of her senses. Critics often call this one of Helen's best books.

Helen, who had a poor sense of direction, could take walks by herself. The newlyweds were deeply in love, and in John, Helen had found the perfect male companion. He functioned as a brother, adviser, and friend—in addition to serving as Helen's literary editor. Under John's direction, Helen wrote what many critics agree is one of her best books, *The World I Live In*.

A Second Memoir

The Story of My Life was a typical memoir, providing a broad overview of the events of her life along with a short section on favorite books and influential mentors. For a long time, Helen's supporters had been asking for a book that described how Helen perceived the world around her. In *The World I Live In*, Helen did just that: She discussed what she actually saw in her mind's eye; described how she functioned in the world using touch, vibrations, and smells; and provided detailed descriptions of her nightly dreams—something readers of the day found particularly fascinating.

Though Helen did enjoy writing *The World I Live In*, she generally had mixed feelings about being a writer by occupation. For one thing, she did not actually enjoy writing—except perhaps toward the very end of her life. Writing was and always would feel like a burden. Moreover, Helen felt that she had written enough about herself and her life. She wanted to write on other subjects: fiction, poetry, politics, and society. However, her publishers and editors told her that people wanted to read about her and her life—not her thoughts on other subjects. Even later in her life, whenever she would write on any subject other than herself, the work would invariably not sell nearly as well as her memoirs and personal accounts.

A Political Awakening

John Macy influenced more than just Helen's writing. He also shaped her powerful political convictions, which would form a major part of her life. Macy was an active **Socialist** and a member of the Socialist Party. Though today in the United States the organized Socialist movement is rather small and not very influential in mainstream politics, in the early days of the twentieth century socialism was quite popular. When Socialist candidate Eugene V. Debs ran for president in 1912, he garnered almost one million votes.

At John's recommendation, Helen read the books of **Communist** founders Karl Marx and Friedrich Engels in German Braille, including the *Communist Manifesto*. As a person who felt excluded from society and occasionally oppressed

Understanding Socialism

The basic tenets of socialism involve the belief that the differences between rich and poor should be minimized, if not eliminated. Everyone should have approximately the same amount of money and property. Socialists believe that one way to achieve this goal is that private property should be discarded and transformed into public property. Moreover, all of the country's resources that generate money—such as quarries, oil wells, mines, and forests—should be publicly held, instead of owned by corporations or private individuals. Most socialists tended to be people who did not hold very much money or power in society, such as **blue-collar workers** who spent their days in mines, in factories, or on farms, as well as the intellectuals, such as Helen and John, who supported them.

This photograph taken in the late nineteenth or early twentieth century shows two Socialist supporters bearing political pennants.

Socialist candidate Eugene Debs poses in this formal portrait. Helen joined the Socialist Party in 1909.

during her life, Helen identified deeply with the plight of poor workers and connected with their struggles. In 1909, Helen joined the Socialist Party of Massachusetts. She made friends with many prominent Socialists and radicals and frequently hosted them at Wrentham.

In addition to her belief in socialism, Helen was also a suffragist. Suffrage was the belief that all people, including women, should have the right to vote. In 1913, most women did not have that right in national elections in the United States.

The Women's Suffrage Movement

Most people today associate the term *suffrage* with the movement to gain women the equal right to vote. In fact, suffrage refers simply to the right to vote—for anyone. However, during the 1910s and 1920s, when Helen was particularly active in the suffrage movement, most of the public's attention was focused around the women's suffrage movement.

During the early years of the United States, only white men had the right to vote. Later, as the idea of equal rights gained popularity, so did the idea that women should be able to cast ballots just like men. In 1869, women's rights leaders began a quest for the vote that would not end until more than fifty years later. The suffragists, or suffragettes as they were sometimes called, wanted Congress to amend the Constitution in order to guarantee women the vote.

Two women march in a suffrage parade in this photograph taken on May 4, 1912. They wear hats and dresses typical of the period, along with sashes supporting their cause. Helen also fought for women's rights.

The movement was controversial. Many people opposed the idea of allowing women to vote and formed anti-suffrage groups. However, the suffragists were undeterred. They organized marches and nonviolent protests in favor of their cause. The women's suffrage movement was ultimately successful. On August 18, 1920, the Nineteenth Amendment was ratified by Congress, which guaranteed women the right to vote.

Only some states permitted women to cast ballots, and then in only limited areas. Helen wrote, "I believe suffrage will lead to socialism and to me socialism is the ideal cause."

Taking a Stand on Social Issues

In 1913, Helen published a series of socialist essays, *Out of the Dark*. Helen wrote about her radical political views in this book, which caused a major upheaval in Helen's image. Her "sweet lady" persona was shattered and in its place was a "militant suffragette," as Helen once described herself to a newspaper reporter. Reporters took note of the transformation, and Helen enjoyed the press she was receiving. Many of the contemporary journalists of Helen's time, however, saw her as a **pawn** of the Socialist Party and the other radical organizations she supported at the time.

Helen also supported the NAACP, a civil rights group. This photograph shows early NAACP participants, including W.E.B. Du Bois, circled below.

Some even considered her brainwashed by Socialists. Helen's family, conservative southerners, was appalled by Helen's political writings and often begged her to keep quiet.

In addition to supporting Socialist causes, Helen was also a supporter of the recently-formed civil rights organization called the National Association for the Advancement of Colored People (NAACP). Though the organization was controversial, Helen was unwavering in her support for their anti-segregation goals. In fact, in 1916 Helen wrote a letter of support with a donation to then-NAACP vice-president Oswald Garrison Villard. W.E.B. Du Bois, then-president, arranged to have the letter reprinted in an NAACP publication. When news came out that Helen was a supporter of civil rights, the Keller family was furious at what they saw as her betrayal of the South and southern values.

Working on Behalf of the Blind

It was also during this period of intense political awakening that Helen embarked on the other great cause of her life: advocacy, or support, for blind people. Helen began serving on the Massachusetts Commission for the Blind, a state organization, writing articles and essays in support of services for blind people.

She caused a particular stir when an article of Helen's appeared in the popular women's magazine, *Ladies' Home Journal*. In the piece, Helen argued for an easy treatment that could prevent many cases of blindness in America—but prejudice and ignorance stood in the way. During the early years of the twentieth century, about one-third of all blindness in infants was caused by an infection called ophthalmia neonatorum. Mothers who were suffering from sexually transmitted diseases passed the infection to their newborns. The infection was easily preventable with eye drops containing a solution of silver nitrate. However, because the mothers were infected by sexually transmitted diseases, both doctors and public health officials preferred to simply ignore the problem.

> It was also during this period of intense political awakening that Helen embarked on the other great cause of her life: advocacy, or support, for blind people.

Helen was appalled by this attitude and shocked that nothing was being done about this problem. In later years, she pleaded with the public to speak frankly about the issue of ophthalmia neonatorum—and its link to venereal disease—to both officials and women themselves. "The day has come when women must face the truth," she wrote. "They cannot escape the consequences of the evil unless they have the knowledge that saves. Must we leave young girls to meet the danger in the dark because we dare not turn the light upon our social wickedness? False delicacy and prudery must give place to precise information and common sense. It is high time to abolish falsehood and let the plain truth come in."

Trouble at Wrentham

Helen's reputation as a writer and speaker was firmly established. Her schedule was always booked and her fame, consistent since she was eight years old, was undiminished. Yet at home at Wrentham, all was not well. Annie's marriage to John was growing strained. The honeymoon glow had worn off, leaving in its place arguments and tension. John began drinking heavily and arguing with his wife, accusing Annie of being too involved with Helen. For her part, Annie worried about John spending too much money—on liquor, travel, fees at his club in Boston, and rent for a city apartment he insisted on keeping. To add to her worries, Annie underwent a serious operation and almost died from complications afterward.

In May 1913, John sailed for Europe by himself for a four-and-a-half-month trip, paid for in part by Helen and Annie. The situation did not improve upon his return. He and Annie immediately resumed arguing, and John began spending the majority of his time at his apartment in Boston. Eventually, he fell to writing bitter and spiteful letters to both Annie and Helen, in which he accused them of conspiring against him. By 1914, the pair permanently separated, and the marriage was over for all intents and purposes. Annie never granted John a divorce. For reasons that are not entirely clear, she would remain legally married to him for the rest of his life and would keep his last name.

CHAPTER 8

Navigating Work and Love

I know enough to realize my dependence upon others. . . . Oh, Teacher, how alone and unprepared I often feel, especially when I wake in the night!

Since Helen's graduation from Radcliffe, she and Annie had lived comfortably at their house in Wrentham, living on the meager and inconsistent funds that Helen earned from her articles and book **royalties**. John's drinking and expensive ways had eaten up much of their savings, and he did not contribute enough to cover their expenses. Moreover, their friends often noted that the two women

Helen demonstrates her keen sense of smell in this photograph.

had no financial sense and spent freely on things like expensive dresses and pedigreed dogs. The Keller family, of course, could not afford to support Helen.

Before John left on his European trip, Annie and Helen decided that they would arrange for a lecture tour. Helen would begin making regular speeches across the country, partly to promote the advancement of blind people but also simply to generate income. However, before the lectures could begin, Helen and her friends agreed that something would have to be done about Helen's eyes. Helen had a lovely face and an attractive figure. She was always perfectly groomed and dressed in fashionable clothes, as she would be for the rest of her life. The problem was that her left eye protruded noticeably, and both eyes were obviously blind. Without telling the public, Helen had an operation to remove both eyes and replace them with blue glass eyes. No one ever found out, and afterward reporters would often refer to Helen's beautiful eyes, never suspecting that they were glass.

Going on the Road

As plans went forward for the lecture tour, Helen continued to work on her speaking voice. Despite the years of practice, her speech was still very hard to understand, and her tone was metallic and hollow, almost mechanical. Helen took regular lessons with a singing teacher to help her gain more flexibility in her vocal range, but on the tour, Annie would have to interpret for her onstage.

Helen gave her first lecture in 1913 in Montclair, New Jersey. The title of the lecture was "The Heart and the Hand or the Right Use of Our Senses." Helen was very nervous, even though Annie stood beside her onstage, translating her words for the audience. At one point, Helen even forgot some of her voice training

This photograph shows Helen perched on the arm of Annie's chair on a porch.

and fled the stage in tears. Still, the audience reception was enthusiastic, and Helen continued on the rest of the tour with renewed confidence.

Enter Polly

In 1913, Annie was forty-seven years old—hardly ancient, yet she seemed older. Her health was very poor, and her ability to get around was becoming limited. Helen and Annie were deeply connected, but they were also realists. They knew it was possible

On Tour

In this excerpt from her memoir *Midstream*, Helen humorously describes the exaggeration in the newspaper articles that were written about her and her lectures.

"We were always amused at the newspaper accounts of our appearance in a place. I was hailed as a princess and a prima donna and a priestess of light. I learned for the first time that I was born blind, deaf, and dumb, that I had educated myself, that I could distinguish [colors], hear telephone messages, predict when it was going to rain, that I was never sad, never discouraged, never pessimistic, that I applied myself with celestial energy to being happy, that I could do anything that anybody with all his faculties could do. They said this was miraculous—and no wonder. We supplied the particulars when we were asked for them; but we never knew what became of the facts."

that Helen would outlive Annie and that both of them might need help as the years wore on. In 1914, they hired an assistant and go-to girl, a Scot named Polly Thomson. Polly lived and traveled with Helen and Annie and performed various secretarial tasks, such as keeping their appointment book and travel schedule. Her energy and organizational skills proved very useful to Helen and Annie during their busy days both on the lecture tour and at home.

In 1916, Helen, Annie, and Peter Fagan, a bright young man they had recently hired as a secretary, made a lecture circuit tour. Polly did not accompany them since she was vacationing in Scotland. This lecture tour was not as successful. America was

RALLY 'ROUND THE FLAG
WITH
UNITED STATES MARINES
"SOLDIERS OF THE SEA"

Your Country Needs You!

Now's The Time to Enlist!

First In Defense On Land Or Sea.
Apply Today At

24 East 23rd Street, New York, N. Y.

Americans were more concerned about war news than attending lectures by Helen and Annie. This recruiting poster from World War I was drawn in 1919 by artist Sidney H. Riesenberg.

gearing up for World War I and audiences had limited attention for anything but war news.

Once the three travelers returned to Wrentham, things grew worse. Annie fell ill and went to a doctor complaining of a cough and a pain in her side. The doctor performed some tests and then gave her the grim diagnosis of tuberculosis. She was ordered to rest. Taking Polly with her, Annie left Helen and spent the winter at Lake Placid, New York. Helen, meanwhile, went to stay with

In this photograph taken in Los Angeles, California, in 1918, Helen sits in the middle as Annie, in black, spells to her. Polly Thomson, hired as an assistant in 1914, is seated at the left.

her sister Mildred and her husband, along with her mother, in Montgomery, Alabama.

Helen in Love

During the 1916 lecture tour, Helen and Peter had spent a lot of time together. At some point they fell in love, but knowing Helen's family would disapprove, they kept their relationship a secret. Thus Helen began one of the most important interludes in her life—not important because of its length, but because of the desires it revealed in herself. Helen was only thirty-six and still in her prime, having lost none of the beauty and freshness of her youth. She was not married and had had no romantic relationships with men, to most biographers' knowledge.

Today, there is a very good chance that Helen would have married if she had wanted to. However, during the early 1900s, the thought of people with disabilities marrying and possibly passing on their "defective" genes to their children was looked upon with revulsion and disgust by much of society. Nevertheless, Helen did not want to be denied the opportunity for marriage—or love.

After Annie and Polly left for Lake Placid, Helen remained at Wrentham for a while before traveling to Montgomery, and Peter stayed with her. Helen and Peter secretly traveled to Boston, where they applied for a marriage license. At this point, Helen decided to tell her mother of her plans to marry, but before she had a chance, a newspaper obtained a copy of the marriage license and published a story about Helen Keller's intentions to marry. Mrs. Keller was furious and confronted her eldest daughter. Helen, caught unawares, denied the relationship—but Kate was unconvinced.

Peter was banished from the Wrentham house and Helen was forced to issue a statement of denial through the family's lawyer, but the Kellers' interference made no difference. She and Peter were still in love and still determined to be together. They made an elaborate plan to elope when Helen traveled with her mother to Mildred's house in Montgomery:

During the 1916 lecture tour, Helen and Peter had spent a lot of time together. At some point they fell in love . . .

Peter would go to Savannah to get Helen as she and her mother switched from a boat to a train there on their way to Alabama.

After stealing Helen away in Savannah, the couple would go by train or boat to Florida, where they would be married. Peter even booked passage on the same boat that Helen and her mother would be on, so he could be ready to take her. However, Mrs. Keller discovered at the last minute that Peter had passage on the ship and took Helen by train to Montgomery instead.

Undaunted, Peter would not give up on his Helen. At one point, he went to Montgomery and met Helen on the porch at Mildred's home, where the two expressed themselves fervently to each other. Mildred spotted the two and called her husband, Warren, who came out on the porch and threatened Peter with a gun. Peter declared that he loved Helen and would marry her, but Warren ran him off nonetheless.

Still, the episode was not concluded. Mildred recalled being awakened one night to hear a noise of someone on the porch outside. When she went to see, Helen was standing there, with a bag packed and dressed for traveling. She was waiting for someone—and that someone was Peter. For reasons no one knows and Helen never revealed, Peter never came to get her though she waited on the porch all night.

Annie Returns

Meanwhile, Annie and Polly had left Lake Placid and traveled to Puerto Rico, where Annie no doubt hoped the warm sun and ocean air would help her recover from the suspected tuberculosis. Helen missed her teacher terribly—they had never been separated for this long before. She threw herself more deeply into her political activities, especially those of a militant Socialist group called the Industrial Workers of the World (IWW). The main Socialist Party had become too slow and bogged down with politics, Helen believed. She wrote articles in support of the IWW

Helen supported the radical Socialist group called Industrial Workers of the World. This photograph shows an IWW demonstration in New York City on April 11, 1914.

and against the United States entering into World War I. The war was simply a way for rich people to make money at the expense of poor people, she wrote.

Finally, in April 1917, Annie and Polly returned from Puerto Rico as America officially entered World War I. Helen was overjoyed to have her teacher back, but more changes were coming. After reviewing their finances, Annie, Helen, Polly, and Mrs. Keller all agreed that the upkeep of the Wrentham house had grown too costly. The place would have to be sold. Everyone, including Helen, was sorry to see the house with its twenty-one acres go. They had made so many happy memories in Wrentham. In its place, Helen and Annie bought a house in Forest Hills, New York.

However, along with the sadness of losing the Wrentham house, Helen and Annie received amazing, happy news: Annie did not have tuberculosis. In fact, she never had it at all—her records had been mixed up with someone else's the whole time. Annie was stout and sickly, but she did not have the dreaded disease. Still, the happy news about Annie and the sale of the Wrentham house did not lift Annie and Helen out of their financial woes. They had to have more money, but where were they going to find it?

CHAPTER 9

The World of Showbiz

It seems strange to me now that I ever had the conceit to go the long, long way to Hollywood, review my life on the screen, and expect the public not to fall asleep over it.

In 1918, Helen had an opportunity to make money in a less conventional way than on the lecture circuit. Hollywood was calling. A historian named Francis Miller had the idea to make a movie about Helen's life.

In those days, movies were still a young art form— only about twenty-five years old. Films were silent and only in black and white. **Intertitles**—also called title cards—appeared with the dialogue on the screen as well as narration of the plot. However, Hollywood was a fast-growing enterprise, and Hollywood's influence on the American public was increasing. Only three years before, a filmmaker named D. W. Griffith had made a big splash with a controversial film, *The Birth of a Nation*. Many people,

A poster for the D. W. Griffith movie *The Birth of a Nation* shows a hooded and robed Ku Klux Klansman riding a horse. Many people found this controversial movie racist.

including the members of the NAACP, found the film racist, but it still made millions of dollars for the studio that produced it.

On the Silent Screen

Helen thought Miller's idea was wonderful. She would star in the movie as herself. However, once the filming of the movie, titled *Deliverance*, started, it was clear that this film would be a *loose* adaptation of Helen's life. In order to appeal to the audience, Miller frequently exaggerated or made up events in her life story. For instance, he and the rest of the movie crew agreed that Helen needed a love interest in the movie—audiences would expect it.

Helen's own silent film, *Deliverance*, is advertised here on this poster from 1920. The film was going to be screened at the Tremont Temple in Boston.

However, Helen had not had a public love affair in real life—at least as far as the directors knew. So Miller invented a love scene that was meant to take place in Helen's mind—in which she would have a romantic encounter with the mythic figure Ulysses. The final scene was just as unbelievable: Helen, who was an excellent equestrian, rode a white horse and blew on a trumpet while leading the people of the world in a sort of triumphal procession.

Helen found the whole experience hilarious and ludicrous and laughed every time Annie described to her what was going on around her and what would take place in the scenes she was about to film. She did not really fit into the glamorous Hollywood social scene either, but she did meet some of the stars of the day, including Mary Pickford, Douglas Fairbanks, and, most notably, Charlie Chaplin, who let her read his lips. *Deliverance* flopped at the box office when it opened in August 1919. Helen and Annie

In this photograph from 1919, Helen reads the lips of Charlie Chaplin, the famous actor and comedian.

Silent Movies

Movies combined with recorded sound—which is commonplace today—were not invented until the late 1920s. Until then, movies had no sound. However, the theaters were far from quiet. The films were almost always accompanied by live music—a sort of old-fashioned soundtrack. Sometimes, one organist or pianist might play along with the action on the screen, but at other times, movies might be accompanied by an entire orchestra.

Early on, silent movies were shot with only one camera, positioned in a corner of the set. Whole scenes were filmed straight through, without the cutaways and camera angles that modern audiences are used to. Right about the time that Helen made her movie, directors were just starting to experiment with using different cameras and angles to film a scene.

Actors also performed differently during the era of silent films. They tended to use a style that modern audiences would consider exaggerated, or overacting: big facial expressions and obvious body language. This was partly because actors needed to convey all sorts of emotion and action without the benefit of dialogue. Many performers of the silent-film era had been stage performers for most of their careers, which called for more exaggeration than acting onscreen. Soon, actors would develop new, more natural styles of acting that worked better for movies.

The famous silent-movie star Mary Pickford poses holding a dog in this still from her movie *Rags*. Helen met Mary while filming *Deliverance* in Hollywood.

still needed money, and Hollywood had not turned out to be the answer.

Stage Stars

The lecture circuit had begun to grow burdensome for Helen and especially for Annie, who was by now middle-aged, very stout, and easily fatigued. The constant travel and effort of giving talks lasting up to an hour and a half had begun to weigh on the pair.

For her entire life, Helen had despised the idea of being treated as a freak or an oddity for crowds to gawk at. Now she was willing to make use of herself to entertain audiences—and make money. Helen and Annie went on the vaudeville circuit in 1919.

Vaudeville was a popular form of entertainment in the latter years of the nineteenth century and the first decades of the twentieth. All sorts of acts came together in what was essentially a large variety show. When attending a vaudeville show, one could be entertained by many different performers, such as dancers, singers, magicians, people reciting poetry, and much more. Vaudeville shows were very popular among middle- and working-class audiences.

The vaudeville schedule was much easier on Helen and Annie. They did not have to travel as

Helen poses backstage in her dressing room at the Palace Theater in New York in 1920, during her time in vaudeville. She and Annie always wore heavy makeup and fancy, glittery dresses.

History of Vaudeville

Vaudeville got its start during variety entertainment shows of the 1850s and 1860s. These shows were mainly comical and were intended for all-male audiences, with the material often naughty and vulgar in nature. Soon, though, organizers realized that by creating shows that had wholesome material, they could attract families—and more paying customers.

Vaudeville shows often lasted for hours. Many of the performers were recent immigrants and showed off skills they had learned in their home countries or that made fun of the trials of living in America. In addition to the popular comic routines, actors would perform plays, musicians would sing or play instruments, and visiting celebrities like Helen Keller would give talks. Many well-known performers got their starts in vaudeville, such as Charlie Chaplin, the Marx Brothers, Abbott and Costello, and the Three Stooges.

With the popularity of radio and film coupled with the great economic depression of the 1930s, vaudeville eventually died out. Audiences could get entertainment right in their own homes with their new radios, and soon theaters began showing movies instead of booking live performers. Sometimes, vaudevillians would perform in between films, but the glory days of vaudeville were over.

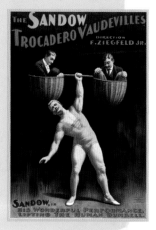

This vaudeville poster advertises a weight lifter called Sandow, performing in the Trocadero Vaudevilles show in 1894.

much as they did on the lecture circuit, and they only performed twenty minutes in the afternoon and twenty minutes in the evening. First, Annie would tell a brief, dramatic story of Helen's early life and describe how she came to know Helen. Helen would demonstrate how she could lip-read, finger-spell, and speak. Then she would take questions from the audience. The pay was handsome—up to two thousand dollars per week at the best vaudeville theaters—and Helen thrived on the work. She loved the energy of the crowd and the enthusiasm of their reactions. The audience loved her back. Helen and Annie made sure they were always beautifully dressed in long, glittery gowns with plenty of jewelry and makeup. They came up with witty, clever quips with which to answer some of the commonly asked audience questions.

She loved the energy of the crowd and the enthusiasm of their reactions.

While Helen loved their new profession, Annie disliked the very vulgarity and showiness of vaudeville that Helen relished. She looked down on their fellow vaudeville performers, thinking that she and Helen were above them. To make matters worse, Annie's eyes, which were always fragile, were irritated by the bright stage lights, and they bothered her almost all of the time.

Gradually, Annie's health grew worse. More and more, Polly accompanied Helen onto the vaudeville stage. As Annie weakened, Polly began serving as Helen's interpreter and assistant in her daily life. In addition to her responsibilities with Helen, Polly also began helping Annie as well. Polly was gradually becoming Helen's public eyes and ears.

CHAPTER 10

Exit Annie

Out of the orb of darkness she led me into golden hours and regions of beauteous thought, bright-spun of love and dreams.

Just before she was due to go onstage one night in Los Angeles in November 1921, Helen received devastating news. Her mother, Kate Keller, had died. In her memoir *Midstream*, Helen called Kate's death "the first bereavement . . . which struck at the very roots of my life." Nonetheless, Helen performed the show as usual, never giving the audience a hint of the shock and grief she was feeling.

By 1924, Annie and Helen's time in vaudeville was drawing to a close. The audiences were diminishing. People who had heard their story once had no need to hear it again. Around this same time, Helen began the work that would occupy her for the rest of her life—fund-raising for the American Foundation for the Blind. The AFB was a new organization working on behalf of the vision impaired. It needed a spokesperson and a face for the public. Helen fit the bill perfectly.

Helen and Annie began making fund-raising speeches for the AFB. At first they spoke in the homes of wealthy people, but they quickly outgrew these venues and began filling churches and other public meeting spaces. Despite her declining health, Annie—rather than Polly—still accompanied Helen to the fund-raising events. After all, the

The American Foundation for the Blind

When Helen began working for the AFB, the organization was only three years old. It was founded by a **philanthropist** who wanted to help the blinded veterans of World War I. Since then, the AFB has been a major force in raising awareness for the vision impaired. Over the decades, the AFB has often focused on promoting products that help blind people navigate through a sighted world. In the 1930s, the organization developed a long-playing record and record player so that blind people could listen to recorded books. Helen Keller helped promote this project, called Talking Books. Talking Books are still produced in modern format by the AFB today. The AFB also lobbied for and was influential in the passage of the Americans with Disabilities Act, the landmark 1990 legislation that guarantees equal rights and equal access for all people with disabilities.

In this photograph c. 1919, Helen walks with a blinded World War I veteran during a visit to the Red Cross Institute for Blinded Soldiers in Baltimore, Maryland.

famous stories were about Helen and Annie, not Helen and Polly. The format of the fund-raising speeches was remarkably like Helen's old vaudeville act. There would be a brief introduction by a foundation staffer. The pair would enter, Annie would describe Helen's education, and Helen would make a speech and answer questions. Then someone would pass around a basket for cash donations and membership forms.

Helen turned out to be an excellent fund-raiser. The AFB had proof when she successfully spearheaded a campaign encouraging manufacturers to donate radios to blind people at very little cost. Helen was not new at either fund-raising or public speaking. She had been working on behalf of others since the days when she had solicited funds for little Tommy Stringer's education so many years before. It was something she was very good at, yet as an adult, the "begging" sat uneasily on her. She often told her friends that she disliked asking rich strangers for charity.

An Author Again

For some time, Helen's publisher, Doubleday, had been encouraging her to write a memoir of her later life. Helen called the book *Midstream* and, just as with most of her other books, she found the writing burdensome and laborious. In addition, she did not have the brilliant pen of John Macy to help her edit, cut, and focus her work this time.

When Doubleday heard of Helen's troubles with the manuscript, they sent one of their editorial assistants—a smart, sensitive young woman named Nella Braddy Henney, to help Helen create her story. Nella arrived at the end of 1926 and actually moved into Helen and Annie's

She often told her friends that she disliked asking rich strangers for charity.

home so that she could work with the author every day until the manuscript was completed. Helen even took a break from fund-raising in 1927 to write the book. Their collaboration was the beginning of what would be a long, though not lifelong, friendship.

By spring 1930, Annie's health was becoming more and more of a concern. In addition to her steadily weakening eyes, she was becoming feeble and irritable. Annie's friends and her doctor thought it would be a good idea for her to go abroad. After some convincing, Annie agreed. However, on the day they were to leave, Annie irrationally refused to budge from her bed at home.

Annie, Helen, and Polly pose in this photograph. As Annie's health weakened, Polly began taking a more important role in Helen's daily life.

Even Helen's pleading could not convince her to board the ship on which Helen, Polly, and she had booked cabins. Eventually Annie was convinced to go on the trip, and after rearranging their ship passage, the trio spent six months in Scotland, England, and Ireland.

Travels Abroad

The trip overseas was the beginning of what would be almost three decades of travel for Helen. For the rest of her active life she would travel throughout the world, making speeches, visiting blind people, and accepting honors and praises. Annie, however, was in a long, slow decline. Surely, Helen and Polly must have realized something was very wrong when in the summer of 1931 Annie insisted on giving away her possessions. But despite her fragile health, the three ladies kept up a rigorous schedule.

After fund-raising in Yugoslavia in 1931, the three women went to Scotland in 1932, where Helen was awarded an honorary doctorate of law degree by the University of Glasgow. Next they went to England where they dined at the **House of Commons**. Helen visited blind and deaf schools and made as many as five speeches a day, which was a strain on her voice even with Polly or Annie interpreting. At Buckingham Palace, the women met King George and Queen Mary, who were much impressed with Helen and Annie's demonstrations of lip-reading. Then, in an attempt to let Annie rest and perhaps recover her health, the trio retreated again to Scotland in 1932.

Polly had arranged for them to stay at an old farmhouse in the Scottish highlands called Arcan Ridge. Annie felt no better, but Helen was in excellent health and spirits. She loved the air and feel of Scotland and adored taking long, rambling walks in the sunshine.

In 1932, the University of Glasgow awarded Helen an honorary doctorate of law degree. She is shown wearing her doctoral cap and gown.

Annie's End

Annie was slowly dying, but she lingered on for several more years. Near the end, she was totally blind, had terrible stomach pains, and was covered with awful carbuncles—large, infected boils on her skin. In a last attempt to bring her joy, Polly and Helen took Annie to Jamaica in 1935. They hoped it would ca July 1936

DOCTORS HOSPITAL
EAST END AVE. AT 87TH ST.
NEW YORK

> For fifty years Anne Sullivan
> Macy, my beloved teacher, has been the
> light in my life. Now she is ill and the
> darkness that covers me has fallen upon
> her; still the light of her love shines
> amid the encircling gloom, and we are
> happy.
>
> Helen Heller

Helen wrote this notice at Doctors Hospital in New York in 1936.

remind her of her beloved Puerto Rico. However, Annie's life was over. She died on October 20, 1936, of heart disease. She was seventy years old. Helen was at her bedside when she took her last breath.

Twelve hundred people attended Annie's funeral in New York. Helen and Polly followed the coffin, clutching each other. Observers noted, though, that Helen spent much of the funeral comforting Polly, rather than the other way around. Annie Sullivan, daughter of illiterate Irish immigrants and former resident of the Tewksbury poorhouse, was cremated and her ashes placed in the National Cathedral in Washington, D.C., the first woman buried there on distinction of her own merits.

CHAPTER 11

Life Without Annie

*. . . I find it even harder to be courageous when,
forgetting, I call Teacher, and only silence answers
me and emptiness touches my outstretched hands.*

After Annie's death, Helen needed time alone to think
about how she was going to live life without Annie.
She needed to get away from the Forest Hills home where
she and Annie lived after selling Wrentham. The house was
too full of memories of her teacher. Soon after the funeral,
Helen and Polly set sail for Scotland to visit Polly's family.
The first few days of the voyage were bleak, as Helen
struggled with overwhelming despair. Nevertheless,
Annie's death, though indescribably painful, was hardly
unexpected. Helen had been mentally preparing for this
moment for a long time.

By the ninth day of the voyage, Helen's appetite,
always good, had returned, and she felt her interest in
reading and thinking return also. Helen could still feel
Annie around her. She felt positive that Annie's presence
was in the train compartment during the journey from
England to Scotland.

While going through her stack of mail in Scotland,
Helen realized for the first time how much Annie had helped
her by editing her letters—skimming and summarizing
some, skipping others. Polly simply read everything to
Helen, who was quickly overwhelmed. Nonetheless, they
were refreshed by their Scottish vacation. Helen and Polly

returned to the United States in February 1936 and settled down to a life without Annie.

Polly differed from Annie in other ways, too, sometimes causing brief arguments with Helen. Polly dressed very well and was fashion conscious. It was important to her that Helen always look her very best as well. Polly insisted Helen wear nice clothes, even around the house. Later in Helen's life, when her hair had become very thin, Polly made Helen wear an uncomfortable, itchy wig that Helen hated. Polly also did not have Annie's intellectual curiosity and wit. So while Polly took care of Helen's appointments and the daily activities of her life, Nella Braddy

The first few days of the voyage were bleak, as Helen struggled with overwhelming despair.

Following Annie's death, Nella Henney and Polly Thomson took care of Helen. The three are shown in this undated photograph: Helen laughs with Nella, at left, and Polly, at right.

Henney, the editor who was by now a close personal friend, took on the task of nurturing Helen's intellectual life.

Visiting Japan

In March 1937, five months after Annie's death, Helen felt ready to resume her traveling life once more. Her first trip proved to be quite an important one, though she did not know it at the time. Helen accepted an invitation from the Japanese government to visit Japan in order to raise money for blind and deaf citizens. Thus began a very close relationship with the people of Japan that would continue throughout Helen's life.

In Japan, Helen gave ninety-seven lectures in thirty-nine cities. She raised more than thirty-five million yen—about $330,000 today. The Japanese people were captivated by Helen. The empress's sister traveled with Helen during her tour, and

This photo from Helen's 1937 trip to Japan shows Helen (left) and Polly dressed in kimonos and sitting on the floor like proper Japanese ladies.

Helen and Polly sit in the study of their home, Arcan Ridge, in Westport, Connecticut, surrounded by some of their many dog companions.

when they visited the Great Buddha of Kamakura, Helen became the first woman permitted to touch the famous statue. One photograph from the trip shows Helen and Polly wearing kimonos on the steps of a building in Tosa Province, surrounded by beaming hosts. Helen is smiling and radiant in her silk robe.

Back in America, Helen and Polly decided to sell the Forest Hills home they had lived in since 1917. It was too full of memories of Annie. They needed a fresh start, and so Helen accepted the donation of a trustee of the AFB to build a colonial home in Westport, Connecticut. They called the white clapboard and green-shuttered house Arcan Ridge, after the farmhouse Annie, Helen, and Polly had occupied during their visit to Scotland. Helen loved the new house and spent many peaceful days there writing and answering letters, gardening and tending her flowerbeds—one of her chief delights. She loved taking walks around the grounds, guided by a handrail built all through the gardens.

Helen's World War II Efforts

After the United States entered World War II in 1941, Helen began the work that she later called "the crowning experience of my life." Helen and Polly traveled the country, visiting wounded soldiers and empathizing with those recently blinded in combat. She helped the soldiers read Braille and joked with them. Many of the young men felt a deep connection with the jolly, laughing, blind-deaf woman: They knew that she knew what they were

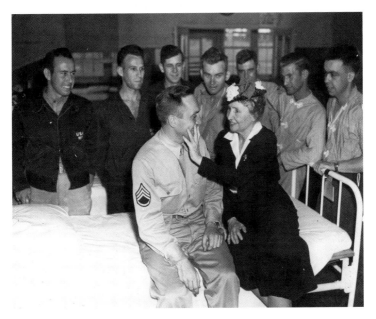

Helen visited many wounded soldiers during World War II. In this photograph from 1945, Helen sits with soldiers at the Moore General Hospital in North Carolina. She is reading the lips of Sergeant Paul Grossman.

going through. Furthermore, Helen was able to show the soldiers that they could still lead rich, useful lives, as she did.

After the war ended in 1945, international travel became safe once more. Helen immediately resumed her world tours for the sister organization of the AFB, the American Foundation for the Overseas Blind. They visited England, France, and Greece, but when Helen and Polly arrived back in Paris they received devastating news from home. A fire at Arcan Ridge, their Connecticut home, had destroyed the house and everything in it, including the manuscript and most of the notes of a memoir Helen was writing about Annie. Polly, who had treasured the house and all of the furniture she had collected, was devastated, but Helen, with her usual calm acceptance, drolly told friends that she was glad to be rid of the dangerous old furnace—the cause of the fire. The house was rebuilt, but Polly always mourned the loss.

Traveling the Globe

From the late 1940s until the 1950s, Helen and Polly maintained a world travel schedule that would have exhausted many younger people. They visited Japan again, where Helen was deeply affected by the devastation caused by the atomic bombs in Hiroshima and Nagasaki. They also went to South Africa, where Helen was given the honorary Zulu name *Homvuselelo*, meaning "You have aroused the consciousness of many." She received an honorary degree from the only integrated educational institution in South Africa, University of the Witwatersrand. Helen supported ending **apartheid** in the country, but she feared a revolt against those she was trying to help—the blind and deaf black Africans— if she publicly spoke out against the system. Later, Helen and Polly visited Israel, Syria, Egypt, Lebanon, and Jordan. Helen met

Impressions of Hiroshima

In this excerpt from a 1948 letter to Nella Henney, Helen describes the painful yet moving experience of visiting the site of the atomic bomb explosion in Hiroshima.

"Polly and I went to Hiroshima . . . to give our usual appeal meeting [Helen refers to the appeal for funds for the AFOB], but no sooner had we arrived than the bitter irony of it all gripped us overpoweringly, and it cost us a supreme effort to speak. . . . Jolting over what had once been paved streets, we visited the one grave—all ashes—where [at] about 8:30, August 6, 1945, ninety thousand men, women and children were instantly killed. . . . The suffering caused by atomic burns and other wounds is incalculable. Polly saw burns on the face of the welfare officer—a shocking sight. He let me touch his face, and the rest is silence—the people struggle on and say nothing about their lifelong hurts."

This photo shows the devastation of the city of Hiroshima, Japan, after the atomic bomb was dropped.

In this photograph c. 1951, Helen stands with members of the Zulu tribe in South Africa during one of her many trips on behalf of the American Foundation for the Overseas Blind (AFOB).

Golda Meir, who was then minister of labor of Israel, and David Ben-Gurion, the prime minister.

By the end of the war, both Polly and Helen were elderly women, and though Helen's health was excellent, as it always had been, Polly's was not. She had extremely high blood pressure, and while in Japan she had suffered a small stroke. Yet despite the admonishments of their friends and Polly's doctor, the two refused to reduce their travel schedule. As Polly returned from their world trips more and more fragile, friends, especially Nella, became highly concerned about what would happen to Helen should Polly die.

Moreover, Polly was terribly protective and possessive of Helen, to the point of obsession. She frequently restricted Helen's

Helen and Polly pose in this formal portrait from 1950. Polly became very protective of Helen during the last years of Polly's life.

visitors, especially when she felt Helen was not looking her best. She refused to let anyone communicate directly with Helen when she was there—even though many of Helen's friends knew the manual language. Everyone worried that Polly's possessiveness made it impossible to train a replacement aide.

A Dance Documentary

In 1952, Helen was still going strong, and she was invited to appear in a film with the famous modern dance pioneer Martha Graham. This film, *The Unconquered*, was meant to be a documentary of Helen's life, and one scene had her appearing

The camera captures Helen standing in the middle of Martha Graham's dancers as she senses their movements.

with Graham. In the scene, Helen stood in the middle of a circle of dancers, "feeling" the dance, while Graham and her dancing performers twirled about. Helen loved the whole experience and felt very close to Graham, who in her creative spirit reminded Helen of Annie.

After completing the film, Helen resumed work on her memoir of Annie. Her initial work on the manuscript had been destroyed in the Arcan Ridge fire many years before. This time, Helen, ordinarily so healthy and robust, found that the writing took a toll on her, mentally and physically. She started suffering from insomnia, a condition that kept her from sleeping, and eczema, a type of skin rash. She was also tired a great deal of the time. Still, she felt driven to record her thoughts about Annie. The completed book, *Teacher*, was published by Doubleday in 1955. Helen was satisfied with it, but some critics wrote that it was too poetic for a biography and merely romanticized their relationship. Others felt it did not deal realistically with the challenges of Annie's life with Helen.

Polly's Death

Everything changed on September 26, 1957. On that day, Polly suffered a severe stroke while at home in the kitchen with Helen. When Polly collapsed, Helen managed to ease her safely to the floor. She could tell what had happened by the throbbing of the pulse at Polly's temple, but she had no way of calling for help. Two and a half hours later, the mailman saw the back door open and came in to find Helen crouched next to Polly on the floor.

Although Polly's stroke was severe, she did not die that day, but she did suffer brain damage. When Polly returned home from the hospital, two caretakers came to live with her and Helen. But even with the help of Winifred Corbally, a nurse, and Evelyn Seide, an AFB secretary, Polly never recovered fully. Instead, she became increasingly angry, unpredictable, and paranoid. Believing that Helen was hers and hers alone, Polly also became furious if anyone paid attention to Helen. She would not even allow Winifred or Evelyn to spell to Helen. Polly died on March 21, 1960, at age seventy-six. She had been with Helen for forty-six years—more than half of her lifetime.

CHAPTER 12

Slowing Hands

I believe that all through these dark and silent years, God has been using my life for a purpose I do not know. . . . But one day I shall understand and then I will be satisfied.

In 1960, Helen was eighty years old. Her hair was thin and white, and her fingers were bony and wrinkled. Helen's hands were becoming less sensitive, and she may have even misunderstood words when they were spelled to her. Even though she was very old, Helen was still living an active life. Her new caretakers, Winifred and Evelyn, were very different from Polly Thomson. They were not particularly elegant women, and they were unconcerned about keeping Helen stylishly dressed. They wanted Helen to enjoy herself—and Helen did.

Sometimes, Helen would get Winifred to take her to the local food stand for a hot dog, which she loved and which Polly would never allow. She would also drink a few martinis—her favorite—before dinner. Helen's house in her later years was a warm and friendly place, with a lot of laughter and a relaxed atmosphere.

The Miracle Worker

All through 1959 and 1960, a new play was running on Broadway. It was called *The Miracle Worker*, and it was the latest attempt to tell Helen's life story. Written by

In this picture, an elderly Helen sits with the young actress Patty Duke, who played Helen as a child in *The Miracle Worker*.

playwright William Gibson, the title refers to Annie Sullivan, who was portrayed as the heroine of the story. The famous actor Anne Bancroft played Annie Sullivan and a child star named Patty Duke played Helen. The play was a smash hit and ran for about seven hundred performances on Broadway. In 1962, it was made into a hugely popular movie.

Helen was amazed by the project and its success, but she always doubted that any drama could convey the depth of her relationship with Annie. *The Miracle Worker* also had a serious effect on Helen's life—it was possibly one cause for the ending of Helen's relationship with her faithful friend and advisor Nella Henney.

The Miracle Worker on Stage and Screen

The Miracle Worker depicts Helen's early life with Annie, when she was first learning the meaning of language. The play is memorable for its gritty scenes of struggle between Annie—played by Anne Bancroft—and Helen—played by Patty Duke. In order to be realistic, the scenes had to appear as violent on stage and screen as they were in reality. Patty Duke had to wear shin guards and kneepads, and both actresses had to actually strike each other in the face. Patty Duke later remembered that one of the hardest parts of performing the role of Helen was that she had to act with her eyes open and staring, as Helen did. During all of the fighting and emotional scenes, she could not change the expression in her eyes.

The scene that has remained strongest in the public's mind over the years is the famous moment by the water pump. Helen holds her hand under the flowing water while Annie works the pump and spells into her hand. With a dramatic flourish, Helen's face lights up and she spells *water* back into Annie's hand. In that moment, the play implies, Helen is transformed from a wild little animal into a thinking person.

In the famous water pump scene from *The Miracle Worker*, Annie, played by Anne Bancroft, attempts to communicate with Helen, played by Patty Duke.

The exact reasons for the break are not entirely clear. Some biographers have speculated that Helen and Nella had a disagreement about the royalties for *The Miracle Worker*. The play was based partly on a biography Nella had written about Annie, so Nella may have felt she was entitled to part of the royalties. Perhaps Polly Thomson, in her paranoid state before she died, spread some sort of rumor to Helen about Nella. Other historians speculate that Helen was simply becoming angry and impatient with her "handlers" as she got older. After a life controlled at least partially by others, maybe she was lashing out, and Nella was simply a good target. In any case, Helen wrote Nella a brief, frosty letter stating that she did not want to see her anymore, and that she was revoking the **power of attorney** she had granted Nella in 1948. What's more, she rewrote her will so that Nella was no longer the literary executor of her estate.

Retreating from Public Life

In October 1961, Helen had a slight stroke, followed by several other strokes. She developed diabetes, and lived for another seven years. She spent her days in bed or in a wheelchair. Sometimes she did not even feel strong enough to be read to, for the first time in her life.

Nevertheless, in 1964 Helen received the Presidential Medal of Freedom, the nation's highest civilian honor, from President Lyndon Johnson. She was so frail, though, that many believed she was not actually aware of what was happening.

In October 1961, Helen had a slight stroke, followed by several other strokes.

Helen died at home in her sleep on June 1, 1968, a few days after suffering a heart attack. She was eighty-seven years old. Winifred told the *New York Times* that Helen just drifted off. Helen's remains were cremated, and though she had requested and arranged for a Swedenborgian funeral, her family disregarded those wishes and held a nondenominational service instead. The service, accompanied by the Perkins School choir, was held at the National Cathedral in Washington, D.C., where twelve hundred mourners were in attendance, including Supreme Court Chief Justice Earl Warren. Helen's ashes were interred next to Annie's and Polly's.

Helen Keller's Legacy

The obituary published in the *New York Times* states, "[d]espite the celebrity that accrued to her and the air of awesomeness with which she was surrounded in her later years, Miss Keller retained an unaffected personality and a certainty that her optimistic attitude toward life was justified."

"I believe that all through these dark and silent years, God has been using my life for a purpose I do not know," Helen is quoted as saying. "But one day I shall understand and then I will be satisfied."

Who knows what kind of a life Helen Keller might have lived had she not been deaf and blind? She probably would have been a typical woman growing up at the turn of the century, smarter than most, perhaps, maybe married with children and a household to run. She might not have been a Socialist, an activist, a suffragist, and a world traveler. Did Helen take on these roles because she was blind and deaf, or in spite of being blind and deaf? No one can ever know.

". . . Miss Keller retained an unaffected personality and a certainty that her optimistic attitude toward life was justified."

Helen's legacy lives on in the Alabama quarter, which is engraved with Helen's image and her name in Braille.

However, the purpose of Helen Keller's life is clear: Through her tireless work on behalf of blind and deaf people, those with disabilities living today have gained greater acceptance in the community. Because Helen refused to live a life of quiet seclusion, the world saw that a blind-deaf woman could write, argue, travel, and influence thousands. Helen laughed in the face of obstacles that would have beaten another person into submission. In doing so, she has enabled generations with similar afflictions to laugh and excel beyond their wildest dreams.

Glossary

apartheid—an official policy of racial segregation formerly practiced in South Africa, involving political, legal, and economic discrimination against nonwhite people.

blue-collar workers—manual or industrial workers, as opposed to "white-collar" office workers.

Communist—a person who believes in communism, the system of social organization in which all property is owned communally, rather than by individuals.

guttural—having a harsh, grating quality, as of sounds produced at the back of the throat.

House of Commons—the lower house of Parliament in England, whose members are elected. In the upper house, the House of Lords, members inherit their positions.

intertitles—title cards used in silent movies that showed dialogue. Words on an intertitle would be shown after a scene was shown, not simultaneously like today's subtitles.

lyceum—an institution or association for popular education or literary debate.

mute—incapable of speech; silent.

opium—a bitter, yellowish-brown narcotic drug prepared from the dried juice of the poppy plant.

patrons—persons who support either a charity, a cause, or a talented person, usually with money or gifts.

pawn—someone who is used or manipulated to further another's purposes.

philanthropist—a person who seeks to increase the well-being of humankind through acts of charity or large donations.

plagiarism—the act of copying someone else's ideas or writings and passing them off as one's own.

poultices—soft, moist cloths, bread, or herbs applied hot to soothe an inflamed or aching part of the body.

power of attorney—a written document given by one person to another, authorizing the latter person to make decisions for the former person.

prodigy—a gifted young person having exceptional qualities or intellect.

quarantined—a period of isolation imposed to halt the spread of disease.

Reconstruction—the period during which states that had seceded during the Civil War were controlled by the federal government before being readmitted to the Union.

royalties—a portion of the income from a work, such as a book, movie, or song, that is paid to the author or creator.

Socialist—someone who supports socialism, the belief that wealth should be equally shared among rich and poor.

tuberculosis—an infectious disease that can affect any tissue in the body but occurs most often in the lungs, characterized by the coughing up of mucus, a fever, weight loss, and chest pain.

valedictorian—the student with the highest ranking in a graduating class.

Bibliography

Books

Herrmann, Dorothy. *Helen Keller: A Life*. New York: Alfred A. Knopf, 1998.

Keller, Helen. *Midstream: My Later Life*. Garden City, NY: Doubleday, 1929.

Keller, Helen. *The Story of My Life*. Garden City, NY: Doubleday, 1924.

Keller, Helen. *The World I Live In*. Edited by Roger Shattuck. New York: New York Review Books, 2003.

Klages, Mary. *Woeful Afflictions: Disability and Sentimentality in Victorian America*. Philadelphia: University of Pennsylvania Press, 1999.

Kleege, Georgina. *Blind Rage: Letters to Helen Keller*. Washington, DC: Gallaudet University Press, 2006.

Lash, Joseph P. *Helen and Teacher: The Story of Helen Keller and Anne Sullivan Macy*. New York: Delacorte Press, 1980.

Nielsen, Kim E., ed. *Helen Keller: Selected Writings*. New York: New York University Press, 2005.

Articles

Crow, Liz. "Helen Keller: Rethinking the Problematic Icon." *Disability & Society* 15, no. 6 (2000): 845-859.

Quickie, J. C. "'Speaking Out': The Political Career of Helen Keller." *Disability & Society* 3, no. 2 (1988): 167-171.

"The Story of My Life," *Atlanta Constitution*, July 5, 1903.

Whitman, Alden. "Triumph Out of Tragedy." *New York Times*, June 2, 1968.

Web Sites

"American Masters: Vaudeville." PBS. http://www.pbs.org/wnet/
    americanmasters/database/vaudeville.html

Dickens, Charles. *American Notes for General Circulation*. Project Gutenberg,
    2006. http://www.gutenberg.org/dirs/etext96/amnts10.txt.

"Helen Keller." Perkins School for the Blind, http://www.perkins.org/
    culture/helenkeller/.

"Louis Braille Biography." American Foundation for the Blind, http://www
    .afb.org/braillebug/louis_braille_bio.asp.

Wolf-Wendel, Lisa. "Single-Sex Institutions." *Education Encyclopedia*. http://
    education.stateuniversity.com/pages/2420/Single-Sex-institutions.html.

Source Notes

The following list identifies the sources of the quoted material found in this
book. The first and last few words of each quotation are cited, followed by the
source. Complete information on each source can be found in the Bibliography.

Abbreviations

HT—*Helen and Teacher: The Story of Helen Keller and Anne Sullivan Macy*
HKRPI—"Helen Keller: Rethinking the Problematic Icon," *Disability
    and Society*
ANGC—*American Notes for General Circulation*
HKL—*Helen Keller: A Life*
MMLL—*Midstream: My Later Life*
SML—*The Story of My Life*
    Note: *The Story of My Life* is composed of a memoir written by Helen Keller
    and a supplementary addition of letters written by Keller and an account by
    Annie Sullivan of Keller's education. Therefore, the author of a quote from
    The Story of My Life will sometimes be listed as "Sullivan."
SMLAC—"The Story of My Life," *Atlanta Constitution*
WLI—*The World I Live In*
HKSW—*Helen Keller: Selecting Writings*
TOT—"Triumph Out of Tragedy," *New York Times*

INTRODUCTION: Commencement
PAGE 1 *"College has breathed . . . aspects of the old ones."*: HT, p. 315

CHAPTER 1: Life in Darkness
PAGE 2 *"[T]his child has . . . reach her mind."*: HKRPI, p. 846
PAGE 4 *"severe congestion . . . stomach and brain,"*: HKL, p. 9
PAGE 4 *"brain fever."*: HKL, p. 9
PAGE 9 *"this child has . . . reach her mind."*: HKRPI, p. 846

Image Credits

About the Author

Emma Carlson Berne has written and edited more than two dozen books for children and young adults, including biographies of such diverse subjects as William Shakespeare, Sacagawea, Frida Kahlo, Snoop Dogg, and Christopher Columbus. She lives in Cincinnati, Ohio.

Index